A Circle
of
Love

BY *Grace H. Ketterman, M.D.*

How to Teach Your Child About Sex
The Complete Book of Baby and Child Care (Revised)
You and Your Child's Problems
You Can Win Over Worry
Before and After the Wedding Night
199 Questions Parents Ask, Answered by Dr. Grace H. Ketterman
A Circle of Love: The Meaning, Making, and Mending of
 Parent-Child Relationships

Grace H. Ketterman, M.D.

A Circle of Love

How You Can Nurture
Creative, Caring,
and Close-Knit
Parent-Child Relationships

Fleming H. Revell Company
Old Tappan, New Jersey

Library of Congress Cataloging-in-Publication Data

Ketterman, Grace H.
  A circle of love.

  1. Parent and child—United States.   2. Parenting—United States.   3. Parent and child—Religious aspects—Christianity.   I. Title.
HQ755.85.K48   1987   306.8'74   86-26128
ISBN 0-8007-1514-4

Copyright © 1987 by Grace H. Ketterman, M.D.
Published by the Fleming H. Revell Company
Old Tappan, New Jersey 07675
Printed in the United States of America

CONTENTS

Introduction   9

PART I   WHAT IS A HEALTHY PARENT-CHILD RELATIONSHIP?   15

1 **The Role of Creativity**   19

(*Biological Creativity; In Discipline and Training; Individualizing Creativity; Follow Your Instincts; Creativity in Role Modeling; Creative Fun; You Form the Environment*)

2 **The Importance of Protection**   23

(*Find the Right Balance; Be Conscious of the Child's Limitations; Know the Child's Capabilities; Be Aware of Dangers; Separate Parental Needs From the Child's; Remember the Child's Individuality*)

3 **Kinds of Nurturing**   29

(*Physical; Intellectual; Social [Interpersonal] Preparation; Emotional Nourishment; Spiritual Nurture*)

4 **The Parent as Educator**   39

(*Parents, First Teachers; Unconscious Teaching; Education for Life; Education Through Training and Discipline*)

5 **Playing and Working Together**   46

(*Working as a Team; Playing Together; Sharing Activities at Various Ages; Balances in Sharing Activities*)

6 **Learn the When and How of Relinquishment**   52

(*Child to Adolescent Point; Adult to Senior Citizen Point; Returning Point*)

Contents

PART II HOW TO BUILD A HEALTHY RELATIONSHIP   59

7 Acquire the Building Skills   63
(*First, You Need a Blueprint; Needed: A Strong Foundation; Also Required: A Solid Frame; Keep Your Perspective; Allow Enough Time*)

8 Use Only Quality Materials   72
(*The Child and Great Expectations; The Need for Good Counsel; Faith a Requirement*)

9 Building Demands Hard Work   78
(*The Discipline of Priorities and Time Allotment; "Explore Rather Than Expect"; Keep a Positive Attitude; Find the Balance in Intimacy and Individuality; Letting Go Is Hard to Do; Make a Firm Commitment; Learn Clear Communications; Grow Through Sharing Activities; Worship: An Important Building Block; Strength in Cultural Events; Relationships Formed Through Crises*)

10 Steps Toward Intimacy   103
(*Ritual; Pastiming; Withdrawing; Ultimate Goal: Intimacy; Be Understanding and Forgiving*)

PART III WHAT CAN DAMAGE A PARENT-CHILD RELATIONSHIP?   111

11 Intellectual and Psychological Causes   115
(*Misunderstandings and Wrong Information; Misinterpretations of Behaviors; Mistaken Identity; Psychological Defense Mechanisms; Unrealistic Expectations; Confusion of Roles; Unhealthy Competition: The Family Triangle*)

12 Emotional Causes of Broken Relationships   136
(*Fears; Anger; Guilt; Ambivalence—Mixed Feelings; Parental Immaturity; Atypical Emotional Problems; Inability to Relinquish the Child; Failure to Be a Place for Returning; Conclusion*)

Contents

PART IV   HOW TO MEND BROKEN RELATIONSHIPS   149

13 **Types of Rifts**   153
(*Temporary; Long-Term or Permanent*)

14 **Healing Through Awareness and Responsibility**   156
(*Steps That Mend; Rectifying Misunderstandings; Clarifying Misinterpretations; Correcting Mistaken Identities; Tearing Down Your Defenses; Straightening Your Crooked Thinking; Breaking the Family Triangle*)

15 **Utilizing the Traits of Healthy Relationships**   171
(*Creativity; Nurturing; Protecting; Educating; Playing; Releasing; Returning Point; Forgiving; Tenacity*)

  A Parent's Prayer   191

INTRODUCTION

As Mother finished the story of Rhoda and the potatoes for the one hundredth time, she looked down lovingly into my rapt four-year-old face. How much I loved my mother and reveled in the great repertoire of stories she told me—stories of her childhood on the prairies of Kansas, stories from her most cherished Book, the Bible, and stories she created to both teach and entertain my inquisitive mind!

"You're beautiful!" I told Mother, and I really felt that she *was* beautiful because we loved each other. But she replied, "I'm not beautiful. I have such a bad complexion!"

My tender heart earnestly wanted to comfort her so I quickly reassured her, "But you wouldn't be Mama without those bumps!" To my surprise, tears filled her eyes and coursed down her cheeks. I now understand those tears were prompted by her grateful response to my childish wish to make her feel better.

When I recall the immensity of my joy and love at that time, I can hardly believe the drastic change that took place in that relationship only a year later.

It was when I was five that I awoke one May morning and skipped downstairs to find a new baby sister had entered my happy world. Strangely enough, I had no awareness that she was expected and knew with sad intuition that things would never again be the same. This gorgeous intruder, I sensed, had usurped my place in the hearts of my entire family. I was afraid, hurt, and resentful, but I had no words with which to express these intense emotions. I tried to be happy, but I felt numb, lonely, and terribly displaced.

To make matters worse, as this beautiful baby began to grow up, I was expected to play with her and make *her* happy. But how could I do that when my misery was so acute? When I complained or acted grouchy, my mother would say, "I always wanted a baby sister. I should think you would be glad to have such a nice child to play with." So, added to my sense of rejection was the loss of understanding from my mother, and a growing sense of her disapproval. The wedge that developed between us grew into a horrible barrier that lasted throughout the rest of our lives.

Those poignant memories are typical of all too many parent-child relationships. They start out so simply and beautifully, but events and emotions shape them with tragic frequency into ugly caricatures of their beginnings. As Dr. Haim G. Ginott says in *Between Parent and Child:*

> No parent wakes up in the morning planning to make his child's life miserable. No mother says to herself, "Today I'll yell, nag, and humiliate my child whenever possible." On the contrary. In the morning many mothers resolve: "This is going to be a peaceful day. No yelling, no arguing, and no fighting." Yet, in spite of good intentions, the unwanted war breaks out again. Once more we find ourselves saying things we do not mean, in a tone we do not like.
>
> All parents want their children to be secure and happy. No one deliberately tries to make his child fearful, shy, inconsiderate or obnoxious. . . .

As in my own experience, those spoilers of loving relationships come unbidden and even unrecognized. Something happens, and a person instinctively reacts. The other reacts to the first person's reaction, and an emotional battle transpires. When such battles continue regularly, estrangement and even permanent enmity is likely to result.

Having experienced such unplanned and painful estrangement from my own mother, I vowed that I would never make her mistakes. I would never expect my children to want an intrusive baby, I would never lecture or yell at them, and I would always strive to understand their feelings.

As each, in turn, entered our hearts and home, I loved them tenderly, rejoiced in every new sign of the development of their bodies and minds. I could never find enough time in my busy life to enjoy them enough.

So why, at fourteen, did Kathy, my oldest daughter, start to seem so remote? Why could I no longer communicate with her? And why did she act as if she could hardly tolerate my presence?

In thinking about the emerging struggle between us, I agonizingly relived my own childhood. Surely I had not made the tragically hurtful mistakes of my mother. I rarely yelled, I usually understood, and I always craved a warm intimacy with my children.

One day as Kathy and I were walking down the mall of a large shopping center, we were enjoying an all-too-rare sense of fun. I recall none of the rest of that conversation, but I vividly recall hearing with the intensity of a thunderbolt, "Mother, I don't think you yell at me enough!"

What wisdom our children have, if we only listen and recognize it. Kathy was right! I had tried so hard to rework my own childhood that I almost missed what my child most needed: a firmer approach in the discipline of her life.

My mistakes cost my children a great deal of needless difficulty, just as my mother's did for me. While she yelled and lectured too much, I was so gentle my children got by with too much misbehavior.

The exciting lessons I learned from my children were these:

1. The difficulties in our relationships were initiated by me, but they created pain for both of us.

2. If I kept a searching mind and a loving heart, I could eventually discover those mistakes.

3. As I unraveled my errors and looked at myself honestly, I could change.

4. My children learned to feed into our relational problems, but as I changed, so did they.

5. My children craved a positive relationship at least as much as I did.

6. They were more than willing to forgive me and in the marvelous ways of children, did not hold grudges.

With time and effort, complicated by backsliding and new goofs, I have become friends with each of my children. I can think of no barriers in our relationships. I know they care about my joys and cares as I do theirs. We are each there for the other through all the experiences of our lives.

Not only have I personally struggled through the problems of several generations of parent-child relationships—with all of the joys and pain—but I have also shared these problems with hundreds of other families. In my work as a pediatrician and child psychiatrist, much of my energy has been focused on analyzing and alleviating those disturbed relationships.

It is exciting to be able to say with certainty that you, too, can solve the problems in your family relationships. You can stop the anger and fighting, the rejection and withdrawal, the guilt and remorse that typify troubled parent-child relationships. And you can replace these with love and laughter, sharing and encouraging, warmth and intimacy.

These chapters will help you discover where your tangles originated, and how you may correct them. You, too, can rejoice in loving, healthy parent-child relationships.

(I assure my readers that I carefully avoid using any identifiable examples from among my patients. All names are fictitious and the stories, while basically true, are disguised to protect the privacy of people.)

PART I

WHAT *IS* A HEALTHY PARENT-CHILD RELATIONSHIP?

Greta's blue eyes filled with tears as she told me about her friend Tish. They had played, argued, and studied together for five years. Almost as close as sisters, they shared intimately in each other's lives.

Now Greta's tears were for the sadness of her friend. Tish's parents were getting a divorce. The relationships among all of the family were severely damaged as loyalties were divided, fear and anxiety mounted, and grief pervaded their lives.

Ideally, every family should have two parents in the household—but the facts are far different. *Newsweek* (July 15, 1985, pp. 42–50) predicted that by 1990, almost half of the families in the United States will be headed by single parents. And that figure fails to measure the pain of pieced-together families who have survived the heartache of divorce and are heroically trying to create a new entity with his-hers-ours children.

The increasing frequency of divorce over a period of decades has created a generation of young parents who have a confused concept of healthy family living. Many of these parents grew up in homes where the single mother had to work and often had little energy for fun or warmth with the children.

Fathers from these divided families often found it easier to try to establish a new life for themselves, or married again, focusing their energies on the building of a new family. Children rarely found the healing for their grief so sorely needed because their parents were too troubled to recognize their children's needs and often no one else was available.

There are six distinctive qualities that not only characterize healthy parent-child relationships but also define the roles of good parents. In this section we will describe and discuss each of these.

Of course, many divorced parents do reach out to their children with comfort, explanations, and reassurance. Even at their best, however, broken homes leave scars that disfigure the new families being constructed. *All* parents need to understand the importance of solid relationships, but it is especially for people who were deprived of happy, positive role models that we need to clearly define healthy parent-child relationships. By recognizing the characteristics of positive intercommunication, a fresh infusion of health may rejuvenate families in general. Individual parents and children, at least, can find new intimacy or recapture that early instinctive warmth of parents and children. The suggestions given here may be a means to healing or they may be preventive, heading off troubled times in the future.

–1–
THE
ROLE OF
CREATIVITY

There are several qualities that are necessary ingredients in making strong and healthy parent-child relationships. Whether you are an intact family, a single-parent, or a blended one, these traits are important to you. The first characteristic is that of creativity.

Biological Creativity

The very existence of a parent-child relationship demands the ultimate creativity. With the birth of each of my three children, I experienced a reverence for life and its original creation that I had never known before. The miracle of the new life that begins with two microscopic cells united through the love of a husband and wife was (and is) awesome. As Psalm 139 says so eloquently: ". . . thou hast covered me in my mother's womb. . . . I am fearfully and wonderfully made: marvellous are thy works . . ." (vs. 13,14).

Whether that new life was born to you or entered your home through the process of adoption, you too have experienced that unique thrill of the creation of life and a new relationship.

In Discipline and Training

All too often, however, people file away that experience of maximum creativity and fail to discover its existence in the rest of their lives. And they especially fail to recognize its value in the training and discipline of their children. Parents typically fall into the grooves that were carved by their mothers or fathers, or they slip into the opposite extreme. Just as I avoided yelling at my children because I was so troubled by my mother's yelling, so do most parents have reactions of some sort against their parents. Or, on the other hand, they believe their parents did such a good job that they set about, knowingly or not, to do the same thing.

I once worked with a father who overpunished his children, especially his son. As we explored the reasons for this, it became clear that this man believed himself to be an excellent person and he attributed his success to the severity of his parents' discipline. If it worked so well for him, he decided, it would be just fine for his children. This father failed to exercise his creative abilities and blindly followed the identical pattern of his father. In this case, the father's discipline emotionally damaged his son and spoiled their relationship.

Individualizing Creativity

A characteristic of healthy parent-child relationships, then, is that of being creative. To develop this trait, you must learn to explore. Pretend that your child is someone not even related to you. Think about his strengths and weaknesses—and your own. How can you and he use the knowledge you find to build a loving and constructive rapport—one that will enhance both of you?

Because you have learned this creative means of relating with one child, don't sit on your laurels! The next child will be so different that you will wonder how she came to your family. The exploring process is one that must be repeated for each child. So make it an exciting, rewarding life-style to be curious about each emerging personality trait. Respect and accept it, and then think about ways to keep that quality positive and help it develop toward constructive purposes.

Follow Your Instincts

Just as it is a biologic instinct to conceive and bear children, there is an instinctive sense about relationships. If you have observed pet mothers with their babies, you may have marveled at the creative, successful ways in which they relate with their young. Perhaps people read too much, think too deeply, and react too intensely to their children. Somehow they have lost touch with that God-given instinct. The creativity has disappeared from their interactions.

Healthy relationships, then, depend on restoring that instinctive creativity that was instilled by God the Creator.

Creativity in Role Modeling

While relationships are born and maintained largely through emotions and their expressions, they are lived out in activities. Sharing activities can provide a great opportunity for creativity. In young childhood, there is a strong, natural tendency for the child to follow the parent everywhere and copy everything the adult does.

As young children become adolescents and adults, the parental mannerisms they copied earlier become their own life-style. The way they identify their needs and meet them (or fail to meet them), and the manner in which they express their emotions will closely resemble their parents' habits. When those parental patterns are positive, the new generation is likely to relate successfully; but if there was abuse or inconsistency, the very attitudes the person hated as a child are likely to reappear in his own life cycle. This process is called *internalization,* and it is the reason relationships are marred generation after generation.

You can change destructive old patterns by becoming aware of them, working to break the habits, and replacing them with new and better ones!

Creative Fun

The creative parent will take advantage of this instinctive tendency and cement the relationship with a child even more firmly by making their shared activities fun. Thinking about how to introduce laughter and warmth into everyday activities is not difficult. Pretending to wrap your toddler in soiled linens and putting him, along with them, into the laundry can gain peals of laughter from both of you. Playing a simple game of hide and seek takes little time—only creative thinking—and can make lifelong memories.

Do be careful to avoid carrying any games or teasing too far. Children are quick to sense humor and join the fun, but they are not very good at knowing when the game ends and the resumption of reality begins. Such happy games have often ended in tears or anger through the parent's failure to catch the glimpse of uncertainty or fear in the child, stop the game, and offer the needed reassurance. In *Have You Hugged Your Teenager Today?* Patricia Rushford writes:

Care should be taken, however, that we don't make fun of our children. Teasing can be dangerous from the wrong mouth. Not all kids can handle it. Safety lies in laughing at ourselves, our feelings, and problems. Gently search out the key to unlock the humor in your child. Each teenager is different so HANDLE WITH CARE and PROCEED WITH CAUTION.

Such care applies to children of all ages!

I will warn you that children will be compelled to want to "do it again, Mommy" until you are weary. So be careful to stop such games when you must with forewarning and understanding. A comment like, "Susan, I'd like to play with you much longer because I love to hear you laugh! But I must get this laundry done before your nap so the noise won't disturb you," will usually enable a child to accept the necessary gear shifts of life.

You Form the Environment

The last area of creativity in relating to your child lies in the environment *you* make. I have seen otherwise loving relationships tragically marred by a parent who emphasized the perfection of the appearance of the home. If every detail was not picture-perfect, there was scolding or punishment that made a climate of severe disapproval and anxiety.

On the other extreme, I have seen children whose homes were so cluttered they were ashamed to invite their friends in the house. The children had neither the power nor the capability to create order and pleasantness.

So I recommend that you parents seek the careful balance in keeping your homes as attractive and neat as possible. But *do* balance that with the maintenance of an attitude of comfort and welcome for your child and her friends. Keep the furnishings and finishes of your home such that accidental spills can be cleaned without too much fuss, and make the family policies such that nicer areas of the home are kept separate from play and roughhouse areas.

It's a fact that material things can help or can ruin an otherwise fine relationship, so use your creativity to make your physical environment part of your happy family life.

–2–
THE IMPORTANCE OF PROTECTION

It is relatively easy to see the value of protectiveness in relating to small children. Infants could not survive those first years of life without the parents' watchful care. Yet almost everyone has seen individuals who are social and even professional cripples because they have been overprotected.

Find the Right Balance

In protection and freedom this is extremely important. Depending on how secure you are as an adult, and also on certain circumstances of life, that balance is easier or more difficult to achieve. The success of that balance also varies from one child to another. The exact amount and type of watchfulness one child requires will certainly be too great for another and far too little for a third. This fact need not defeat you, however. It only means that you face the exciting challenge of exploring each child's varying capabilities and fitting your protectiveness to the needs of the individual child.

Once again, I am reminded of the simple lessons God's small creatures can teach. The mother cat and dog have an amazingly clear sense of timing as to when and how to relinquish their fierce protectiveness over their young. Were it not for that carefully preserved instinct, baby animals would mature without the lifesaving instinct of self-protection.

Offering to your child a similar bit of wisdom is one of the secrets of good parent-child relationships. When he is small and unable to defend himself, you must protect him from chemicals, undue heat or cold, the attacks of other children, and the dangers of traffic or nature. As he becomes capable of fighting his own battles, however, controlling his impulses and developing good judgment, you must gradually step back and both teach and encourage him to practice these skills. Eventually, you may need to require him to use these by refusing to take action or be responsible for him. On the other hand, your child should not be afraid to come to you when in trouble. Bill Cosby points out in *Fatherhood* the importance of "being there":

> Just as your children are not afraid to let you know that they are not perfect (they let you know it night and day), you must not be afraid to let them know that you're not perfect too. The most important thing to let them know is simply that you're there, that you're the one they can trust the most, that you're the best person on the face of the earth to whom they can come and say, "I have a problem."
>
> If *only* more kids would say "I have a problem" instead of "No problem."

To provide the right kind and amount of protection demands several qualities.

Be Conscious of the Child's Limitations

A lovely statement from the Psalms says, "Like as a father pitieth his children, so the Lord pitieth them that fear him" (Psalms 103:13). When we define *pity* as Webster does as "sorrow or compassion felt for another person's pain or suffering," then a major part of positive relationships is understood.

One day I watched my three-year-old child learning to button her sweater. After an eternity of waiting, her chubby little fingers had finished the three bottom buttons, only to discover that there was an extra buttonhole left on that side of the sweater. Her eyes revealed the depth of fatigue and frustration in her heart as she patiently unbuttoned those tiny knobs and started over.

How much easier for me it would have been to reach over and do it myself. But I was able to find that healthy pity which shared her frustration but understood her need to "do it myself!" It is such pity that offers a good component of protectiveness. In this situation, it was my child's need to grow in self-confidence and competence that demanded protection—not the difficulty of the present task. Healthy protection must be foresighted if it is to serve the child and the relationship well.

It takes time and careful observation to know each child well enough to understand her limitations. It takes tough love to help her accept and live well within those limits. And it demands great wisdom to know when those limits may safely be expanded. The parent who invests energy in achieving these goals will almost certainly prevent serious rebellion and the breaking of that parent-child bond.

Know the Child's Capabilities

A friend of mine knew his teenage son extremely well. He had carefully observed his progress through school and knew he had a fine mind indeed. Unfortunately, however, the intelligence often failed to be rewarded because of the son's laziness and his strong preference for play!

Realizing that he had only a few months to help his son develop better habits before going to college, this father set a simple goal. He would require this young man to do his last English paper of the semester in a truly fine fashion. He made it quite clear that his son could not have the car for a Saturday-night date until he had perfected that paper.

Early in the afternoon, the student scribbled a fairly good report and prepared to go out as his father carefully read it. My friend needed only to check the first page to see that this was a poor sample of his son's best. He pointed out the flaws and asked for a better job. The next result was better, but far below his son's capability. Yet another version was demanded.

Laboriously, father and son struggled through that seemingly endless afternoon and evening. The date was postponed and the son was furious, but somehow that father persevered. The final product was truly excellent and brought high commendation from his teacher.

This father protected his son from developing habits of carelessness. He cared enough to help that boy overcome laziness and a natural preference for fun!

Healthy protection will risk the temporary disruption of a relationship for the good of helping a child recognize and develop his capabilities to the maximum.

Be Aware of Dangers

Throughout a child's growing-up years, there are dangers that put him or her at risk but which the child may not recognize. A two-year-old loved to play with his grandmother's lighter. It posed a grave risk not only to his safety but also to the house and even her own safety. Yet this grandmother was unwilling to risk her relationship with the child by taking it from him. Her failure to provide protection avoided his anger toward her, but it caused immense anxiety for her daughter, the mother.

A worried-looking mother sat in my office with her sullen-faced teenager. This beautiful girl was dating an older boy, and the mother had discovered they were sharing sexual intimacy. They were being responsible enough to prevent pregnancy, but this exceptionally wise mother saw the real danger in this liaison. She knew that her daughter was engaging in sex in order to maintain a shaky relationship and also realized that sexual intimacy becomes so intense that it prevents the broader and vitally important discoveries and sharing of other activities. She believed the biblical injunction against extramarital sex was (is) based on wisdom and healthy protection.

In spite of her daughter's angry self-defense and rebellious insistence that her relationship was okay, the mother held out. It simply must stop. She gently explained her reasons and offered examples validating her values. The session became intense, and I was unable to predict the outcome as they left.

Several weeks later, I met again with this courageous mother and her lovely daughter. The basic strength of their loving relationship was made extremely clear. Rather than rebelling, this girl finally agreed—simply because she did not want to hurt and worry her mother—to stop the sexual part of her liaison, and her boyfriend agreed.

Several years later I encountered the young woman again. She was happily married to a different man. In reminiscing, she verified the wisdom in her mother's tough love. When she had stopped having sex with the earlier boyfriend, he had soon lost interest in her. Painful as that was, she realized what a frail relationship that had been if it was based on his selfish sexual pleasure.

Healthy parental protection must be alert to dangers that are beyond the awareness of their children. It must teach them of those threats and protect them from the damage even when the children resent it. Childish or adolescent anger at necessary parental protection is to be expected. The mature parent cares enough to accept that anger and await its eventual disappearance. He will accept the temporary interruption of the relationship in order to gain the necessary goal and will eventually earn his child's respect.

Separate Parental Needs From the Child's

Many loving but overprotective parents fall into difficulties due to their need to be needed. That early exuberance at creating a new life can arouse in parents a new joy at discovering their immense importance to this life. If those parents are lacking in an overall sense of healthy confidence, they may learn to gain too much of their satisfaction from the child's need of them.

Such a problem is almost never conscious. Parents do not think, "I have never felt so valued and important in my life as my child makes me feel. Therefore I will keep him or her immature and totally dependent on me so I can feel more and more important!" But that is, in fact, how they relate to the child.

Overprotective parents often talk baby talk to their children for extended periods. They rarely allow them to do things that have even slight risks involved. They tend to do things for the children they could (and should) very well do for themselves. They may lecture and scold, or they may be gentle and patient. The long and short of it is that parents who need to be needed are overprotective, overreactive, and keep their children dependent on them.

On the other hand, I see a growing number of parents who seem to require freedom. They resent the normal dependency needs of their children and allow them privileges they are neither responsible nor wise enough to handle.

This parental need for freedom may extend from infancy to adolescence or it may intrude at various intervals as the children mature. True enough, it is not convenient to be parents. It demands time, energy, and sacrifices and many parents, being unprepared for this, are simply unwilling to sacrifice. In such cases there are varying degrees of neglect that leave even worse damage on the child than abuse.

In Part IV we will discover how to mend the damage such extremes in parents' needs may create. The wise parent will know himself well enough to recognize tendencies toward the extremes of neglect or overprotection. He or she will discuss these feelings with a friend or adviser and find ways to meet his or her own needs that will not damage the children.

Remember the Child's Individuality

Rather than encouraging dependency, or unwittingly neglecting children's needs, it is vital that parents recognize at birth the individuality of a child. Having carried their babies for nine months within their own bodies, mothers are especially likely to have difficulty seeing the child as a separate human being. If the child looks or acts like they do, parents are even more certain to face the risk of overidentifying with the child.

Maureen. It will take conscious effort to avoid or overcome such a tendency. Maureen had been a very sensitive child. She had often suffered from teasing by her classmates but had never discovered how to understand or cope with that teasing.

When Maureen became a mother, she was elated that her daughter was gentle and sensitive as she had been. But she was horrified later when her child was teased by others. Maureen fiercely corrected those friends and protected her daughter carefully against teasing.

It was some years later that Maureen learned her child thought it was fun to be teased. She had enough of her father's humor and her own secure sense of friendliness that the teasing had not bothered her!

As much as your child may resemble you, and no matter how life for him or her may recall memories from your past, he or she is *not* you. Practice, early on, seeing and relating with your child as if he were a brand-new friend who has entered your life. Explore her tastes and interests, observe her movements, appearance, and expressions as if they were totally new. You will learn that such exploring facilitates the growth of the very best qualities in your child and your relationship with that child.

—3—
KINDS
OF
NURTURING

When that baby sister of mine was tiny, I recall awakening frequently at night because she was crying. My father would be walking the floor with her, gently trying to soothe and quiet her. Finally my parents took her to the doctor, who discovered she simply was not getting enough nourishment. She was hungry. He worked out a special formula for her and soon she was sleeping through the night, growing dimpled, chubby, and happy. The physical nurturing is probably the first kind we become conscious of but there are others, also important.

Physical

Due to the discoveries of modern science as well as the shocking pain of world hunger, most people are well aware of the importance of proper nutrition. Yet reaching that goal of the perfect balance of the basic food elements is one of the most common causes of parent-child problems. Parents who unwittingly set up lifelong power struggles often begin those battles over exactly what and how much food John or Sally eats.

Remember that a wise Creator put into each person a well-set regulator of calorie and nutritional needs. By offering the basic foods daily, keeping the relationship loving, and trusting that child's instinctive sense of need, you can avoid useless battles over food.

Intellectual

After long days of very hard work, my parents spent their late-evening hours reading. They read farm magazines, religious periodicals, and whatever books were available. Not only did they read, but they frequently read aloud or commented on the ideas they encountered.

As soon as I could read, I recall investing most of my spare time reading too. In fact, I read so voraciously that I often neglected my household responsibilities. Both my teacher and my parents forbade my reading at all for periods of time in order to learn arithmetic and basic family duties. One of the few times I lost the privilege of playing during recess time was the day the teacher caught me hiding my beloved book in my lap—hoping she would not see me breaking her rule!

Today, I feel confident both the teacher and my parents would agree that reading was mainly a good habit. It fed my mind and motivated me for the many long years of study I had to pursue in reaching my professional goals.

Intellectual nurturing can create another link in the bond of intimacy between parents and children. Seeing those fresh minds develop, encouraging that growth, and interweaving your own intellect with theirs is exciting for both parents and children.

A friend of mine uses his knowledge of nature to whet the intellects of his children. A nest of baby bunnies, a fallen bird's egg, or a thunderstorm are all opportunities to share his knowledge, direct them to a book, or pique their curiosity. There is so much to know! And it's such fun to find out many of the "hows" and "whys"! What a priceless means of moving toward a healthy relationship of mutual respect through intellectual nurturing.

Social (Interpersonal) Preparation

Nurturing a child socially may, at first, seem ridiculous. But in fact it is only when children are fed the interpersonal nutrients of acceptance and respect that they can develop social health. Without these and other healthy qualities in the parent-child relationship, children will develop antisocially or become isolated. Let's take a look at some examples.

Millie. She was eight when I made her acquaintance. She was exceptionally bright but her intellectual capabilities were gravely crippled by her social problems. She belittled other children, refused to follow classroom rules, and failed to complete her assignments. She was rude and selfish, even to the point of stealing if she wanted something belonging to another person.

As we investigated the reasons for Millie's antisocial behaviors, we discovered that she was an only child. Her parents were extremely proud of her fine mind, and perhaps a bit in awe of her. They were, themselves, very self-centered, and neither wanted to endure the inconvenience of teaching their child to respect authority. Furthermore, they preferred their own activities to spending time with Millie. They never invited other children into their home when she was a preschooler, so she had never learned to relate with other children in either a caring or fun-loving manner. Millie had missed out on social nurturing through her parents' neglect.

Failure to spend time together, to provide consistent training and discipline, to laugh and play, read and talk, love and pray together, is the essence of a socially starved child. In his book *Fatherhood*, Billy Cosby writes from his own experience as a parent:

> . . . my wife and I have tried to stay tuned in to him and the girls from the very beginning. We have shown all five of them constant attention, faith, and love. Like all parents since Adam and Eve (who never quite seemed to understand sibling rivalry), we have made mistakes; but we've learned from them, we've learned from the *kids*, and we've all grown together. The seven of us will always stumble and bumble from time to time, but we do have the kind of mutual trust that I wish the United Nations had. And, with breaks for a little hollering, we smile a lot.

Larry. This boy, on the other hand, was extremely shy. He rarely played with other children and withdrew in obvious fear if anyone made a sudden motion near him. He was pale and thin, and his large blue eyes darted fearfully about as I talked with him. I noticed small round scars on his hands and arms. Further examination revealed more of these on his little legs, and he told me there were others on his tummy.

After a long time, Larry told me these marks, some of them

fiery red and festering, were from cigarette burns. The tragic story revealed that his parents had decided to discipline him through the pain inflicted by burning his tender flesh with lighted cigarettes.

Child abuse is a mushrooming plague in our Western society. It is like a toxin—a poison—in the social development of children. It will inevitably result in serious damage, not just to the relationship but to the child himself. It will mar all other relationships in one way or another.

While Larry withdrew from his abusive parents in fear, Millie covered her fear with a rude indifference that kept everyone at a safe distance from her. She learned to retort to her neglectful mother in anger and to get even with her in sneaky ways that enabled her to feel more powerful and less insecure.

To properly nurture a child's healthy social development demands a wholesome parent-child relationship. The ingredients of such a situation are these:

1. *The ability to communicate well.* That means that parents need to talk to a child from birth on. They need to listen to that child and carefully observe his facial expression, his posture, even the way he cries or gestures.

When the child is too young to talk, parents should interpret to him, and for him, what his body language seems to say. And when the child or adolescent can talk, parents must learn to listen. Showing a child the respect of hearing him out in a caring way will keep the relationship a positive one.

2. *A good parent-child relationship is one that demonstrates consideration for the needs and feelings of others.* So many parents fail to realize this applies to the way they relate to their children at home, in church, or in shopping centers. Almost never do I enter my grocery store or any public place without seeing a parent treat a child with anger or downright abuse. When I see children in classrooms treating each other and their teachers with rudeness instead of consideration, then I can be almost certain that that child has been treated by his parents in a similar fashion.

Parents, please feed your child the social vitamins of kindness, good manners, and thoughtfulness for others. You will need to model this as well as teach it by requiring such behavior of your child. I believe behaviors can and must be taught, but attitudes are "caught" through example.

3. *Comfortable parent-child relationships demand some degree of self-confidence.* As parents, value your children and their achievements; as you let them know your pride in them, they will learn to feel good enough about themselves to accept and value others in their relationships.

As Dr. James Dobson says in *Hide or Seek:* "Believe it or not, a five-year-old is capable of 'feeling' his own lack of worth in this system. Most of our little ones have observed very early that some people are valuable and some aren't; they also know when they are one of the losers! In many ways we parents inadvertently teach this system to them, beginning in infancy to place a price tag on human worth. The result is widespread inferiority and inadequacy. . . ."

4. *One of the best ingredients for social health is that of family hospitality.* When parents welcome friends into their home and show warmth and consideration in entertaining people, children will almost certainly absorb that attitude that is demonstrated. This practice affords a unique opportunity to teach children that rare balance in being a part of the adult interaction without being intrusive or monopolizing the attention.

5. *Finally, good social health, so essential to fine parent-child relationships, demands good judgment.* Exposing children to a variety of social situations is necessary, along with careful guidance and parental example, for nurturing them socially. There are obvious and immense differences in the behavior that is proper at a ball game and that to be expected in church or at school. Perhaps all of you can join me in thinking of specific children who seem to have no such discernment.

Therefore, feed your children a variety of experiences; carefully demonstrate and teach them how to behave in each situation. Your relationship to your child will be greatly enriched by developing such skills.

Emotional Nourishment

Shelley. Stubbornly, Shelley sat glaring at her father. She had been getting into trouble with her junior high teachers. Her friends were increasingly selected from students who also were rebelling. Shelley's father was worried. His furrowed brow and anxious eyes clearly told me his deep concern about his beautiful, only daughter. Carefully measuring each word so as to avoid antagonizing her further he asked, "Shelley, why don't you like to talk with me? I see you looking upset and I want to help, but it seems you have trouble opening up to me."

In a rush of emotion, Shelley replied, "Well, Dad, you never talk to me! Why should I always be the one?" Her retort was angry and sounded rude, but it was honest. Her dad verified the fact that he had always been a private person and one who rarely revealed his feelings to anyone, much less his teenage daughter. The exciting ending to this example was the father's willingness to change. As he learned, laboriously, to identify his emotions and share his life with Shelley, her anger and hurt subsided and her love and trust grew.

Parent-child relationships can be purely intellectual, and both people will grow mentally. They may share physical activities and even express physical affection regularly. They may also explore all sorts of social events and learn the best of interpersonal communications and skills. But without the spice of emotional nurturing, that relationship will be dull and uninteresting.

The ability to experience and share emotions is a vital part of a parent-child relationship. I believe the broader and deeper those feelings are, and the more honestly they are communicated, the stronger and richer is that relationship.

Unfortunately, many families, out of old habits, have learned to deny some (or most) emotions, and live on a shallow level in their relationships.

Evelyn. She was an exuberant and outgoing child. Her brown eyes twinkled and her blond hair bobbed as she skipped about with her sister or friends. In her early teens, however, an experience with her father changed all that.

Even in recalling that time many years later, tears welled up and coursed down her face as Evelyn told me her story. On a Saturday afternoon, she was raptly listening to the radio report of her high school's basketball game. They were playing their school's arch rival, and Evelyn was excitedly following every account of the tense competition. As her team made the winning score, she yelled her excitement at the conquest.

To her amazement, her father arose from the chair where he was reading and looked angrily at her. With great sarcasm and harshness he lectured her. He professed amazement that she could have wasted an afternoon listening to the foolishness of a ball game. He could not believe the undignified behavior she, a young lady, had just demonstrated. This, and much more, he unloaded into her astonished ears.

Evelyn, a sensitive girl who wanted to please her father, heard him out, and resolved to show no further emotions—ever. For many years, she stifled and denied feelings, hoping to regain her stern father's approval. When she realized, however, that her resolve was hurting her children and her marriage, she reversed that fateful decision. It took many more years, however, to regain her emotional normality.

Nurturing children emotionally demands the following:

1. *The parents' genuine acceptance of their own feelings throughout the total spectrum—joy/sorrow, anger/peace, love/resentment, concern/indifference, fear/courage.* Whatever your emotions, know that the capacity to experience them is God-given and therefore okay. It is fundamental for parents to understand this fact before they can, through their example, teach children how to recognize and express *their* emotions appropriately.

2. *The freedom to express all feelings positively and honestly is the next essential.* To find a constructive mode for such expression means you must not hide or deny these emotions. On the other hand, you must avoid exploding your feelings in violent ways that will cause hurt and set the stage for retaliation. Recognize and clearly identify each emotion early, before it gets out of control, and determine what has prompted that feeling. Finally, choose what you will do

about the reason, and how and when you will deal with the situation.

3. *Teach your children, both verbally and by your example, how to follow those same steps of: finding names for their feelings; determining why they feel that way; and, finally, working out a solution to the problem.*

4. *Listen to your children's feelings without judging or lecturing.* Be careful to look through the initial feeling to find the very heart of their trouble. As you listen, try to guide them to the solutions rather than hastily solving the problems for them. Many parents react so angrily to their child's rudeness in a disagreement that they totally miss the profound importance of what the child is trying to say!

5. *Be alert to the possibility of using your feelings in a manipulative manner.* Covering concern or fear with anger keeps others confused about the true problem. Conversely, distorting anger to make it look like sadness is equally deceptive. I have seen people who, through years of practice, had so disguised their emotions that they themselves no longer knew for sure what they felt.

Life becomes vibrant and exciting when we learn to recognize, accept, and express (appropriately) all of the emotions of which we are capable. Parent-child relationships are infinitely enriched when parents nurture their own emotional life and that of their children.

Spiritual Nurture

In our increasingly mechanized, impersonal Western world, the need for nurturing the spirit in and through parent-child relationships becomes extremely important.

Unfortunately, many parents seem to believe that spiritual food comes only from church or perhaps from some organized form of Bible study or prayer. These disciplines are important and have enormous value in clarifying and teaching the Truth of the Ages as God has preserved it in His Word.

God, however, puts a higher priority on relationships. Jesus says in Matthew 18:15: "If your brother sins against you, go and show him his fault, just between the two of you. If he listens to you, you have won your brother over" (NIV). Yes, we can learn a lot from God's Word. In Luke 6:27–38 He gives us principles for dealing with others.

But there are some other things that are useful in feeding children's spirits.

1. *Living out your values makes them the most understandable and believable to children.* I spent my childhood in the years of the Great Depression of the 1930s. My mother prayed about money and how it was spent. Even the purchase of a new pair of shoes warranted her supplications that we'd find a real bargain.

2. *Talking about spiritual values should be as natural as the discussion of events at school that day or the dinner menu.* I find a great many families become strangely shy or even tongue-tied when topics of a religious nature come up. In fact, they avoid even bringing up such topics! God is the Source of everything that is worthwhile in life, and it seems incredibly rude to deny His significance by failing to mention Him.

3. *The Bible is replete with references to nature as God created it—* yet how many of His children ignore the grandeur of creation. I have seen a magnificent rainbow as I stopped for a traffic light in the midwestern city where I lived. A glance about me revealed that few pedestrians passing by (and none of my fellow motorists) even saw this glorious sight. It took my grandson's toddler days to remind even me of the excitement and wonder of bushy-tailed squirrels frisking up and down trees or birds flying freely through the air. Nourish your child's spirit by teaching him to revel in the wonders of nature, and let his wonder rekindle your own.

4. *The miracle of the human body itself will awe your child as you help him or her to understand it.* The intricacies of sight, sound, speech, touch, taste, and smell are all examples of the physical functioning that the Creator made to enable us to be inspired by His masterpiece of creation.

5. *More spiritual food can be found in the spirit of other people.* Help your child to learn about heroes who overcame obstacles in life, worked hard to become useful, or endured tragedy or handicaps. One of the heroines of my life was Helen Keller, the girl who was both blind and deaf, yet became an inspiration to millions.

Other heroes are numerous but often forgotten. Abraham Lincoln, Winston Churchill, Clara Barton, who organized the American Red Cross, Martin Luther King—these and many more heroes and heroines are examples of people who rose to greatness. Most of them overcame immense obstacles and personal heartache to achieve their success. All of them were imperfect, but their weaknesses did not stop them!

6. *I urge you to also share the teachings of the Bible with your child, not as a means to chastise or lecture, but as a normal part of your own search for divine wisdom, love, and strength for living.* As Paul wrote to Timothy, "All Scripture is God-breathed and is useful for teaching, rebuking, correcting and training in righteousness" (2 Timothy 3:16 NIV). The Bible is full of more heroes who can become models for you and your children to emulate.

7. *Formal prayers certainly are another wonderful means of nurturing spiritual life.* It was accidentally discovering my father, kneeling for his own private prayers, that profoundly impressed me with the vital role prayer fulfills in life. Be an example to your children.

Spiritual nurturing is of mutual benefit. As I tried to teach my children through prayer, Bible stories, and reveling in God's creation, my own faith grew and I was nurtured spiritually. When one of the children came to me saying, "Oh, Mommy! There's a rainbow! Come see it!" I knew we were sharing really important experiences. And that's the core of truly special relationships.

-4-
THE PARENT AS EDUCATOR

Formal education is a privilege that many young people no longer value. A great majority of the world's people do not have the opportunity to achieve the learning that is so inexpensively available to American youth.

One of the most essential ingredients of education, however, is the parents' attitude and example regarding basic curiosity and a desire to learn.

My parents were able to achieve only an eighth-grade education. Yet they were avid students. My father read everything he could find and shared with us the ideas he gleaned. He read aloud to us children and created a bond of shared interests, ideas, laughter, and even tears through such sharing.

It is not so much the didactic or "book" learning that is important in parent-child relationships, however. It is, instead, educating children about life—and death; about themselves—and others; about their world—and how they fit into it. The love of learning and the curiosity that will *only* be satisfied through finding out about something—that is a parent's means of prompting a child to become wise and to respect and appreciate the teacher.

My parents encouraged my love for learning (and for them) by their examples. The dad who took time out during a busy day to show a little girl a baby chick being hatched, a brand-new baby colt on its first wobbly walk, or a litter of pink squealing piglets did not know the impact those simple sights would have on her life! He was teaching her about Creation, the Creator, and her own place in His scheme of things.

Through my parents' reading, I learned to love books; through their philosophy, I learned to think; through their humor, I learned to laugh; through their discipline, I learned obedience, respect, and self-control. It was through their faith that my own was born.

My parents were burdened with much concern: a large family living through years of economic depression, a war which threatened our world and our own family, a variety of real or potential disasters. Yet they elected to use these troubles as opportunities to learn and grow—teaching us by their examples.

I hope you, too, will learn from their examples. Take time out to teach your children, to share your own experiences, and to learn from them as well!

My father's good humor was a never-failing source of delight, and drew me to him like a magnet. His alertness to the "ordinary" but exciting events of life was matched only by his astute awareness of the value of those happenings in teaching me his wisdom. His patience and quietness taught me the way to wait for the right time. And his restraint and careful explanations made sense to my childish impulsiveness.

Parents, First Teachers

Our Western culture has lost so much of the intuitive roles of parenting that many concerned people are devising new means of teaching those instinctive skills.

A large midwestern state (Missouri) has, in fact, passed a law requiring public schools to offer training in parenting to new parents. At one time in history such an idea would have been ridiculed, but today the in-depth research of highly respected child psychologists reveals the necessity (and the exciting possibilities) of this resource.

People who have themselves been good parents are selected and trained in the best possible methods of teaching. These parent educators are *not* concerned with the teaching of early mathematical concepts to infants or precocious reading skills to toddlers. They are, very simply, concerned with teaching warm, loving relationship skills. Their goal is that of helping parents of new babies know how to understand them, how to bond with them, and what to expect of them. It is the ultimate hope of this project that by teaching parents how to relate with their infants in that intricately balanced blend of tender, tough, and protective love, we may see more children develop into healthy adults.

In sex education, physical development, social skills, spiritual awareness, and, in fact, in every aspect of life, parents are a child's first teachers. For better or worse, like it or not, these are the facts. How important it is for parents to learn how to be really great teachers.

To accomplish the task of great teaching demands the following insights and skills:

1. Thoughtfulness and searching for the basic concepts you want your child to learn.

2. Reviewing your own childhood and the ideas and values that you know turned your life in positive directions.

3. Honesty in discerning the mistakes in parenting that hurt you.

4. Observing other families and reflecting on the interactions that bring about positive relationships and attitudes, and those that fall short.

5. Willingness to admit mistakes and courage to correct them.

6. Ability to explore new ideas and methods and responsibly trying them out.

7. Courage to take the risk of openness in sharing these concepts.

You can become not just *good* teachers as parents but truly great ones!

Unconscious Teaching

Her favorite book was worn and marked on nearly every page with notes, underlining, and tears. My silver-haired mother rarely read anything except that priceless Bible or articles relating to it. Her values, based relentlessly on her absolute conviction of its Truth, was and is an example I cherish. My mother taught me the stories of this Book, but her cherishing of its meaning was such a part of her that I knew it worked. Her best teaching was the example of her absolute faith.

Similarly, my father's unquenchable thirst for knowledge created in me an immense respect for learning. He did not need to urge me to read and study—his conversation prompted profound thinking and searching from my own mind, even as a child.

The ways you walk and talk become the habits of your children. The ways in which you recognize and express your emotions set the mold by which your children's emotions are handled as they grow and the manner in which they will relate to your grandchildren someday.

Education for Life

In today's world there is a massive increase in knowledge that seems certain to grow with even more amazing speed; yet the capacity of people to relate lovingly with each other is seriously declining. *Part of the task of parents is to teach their children how to understand the life skills that are basic to the world in which they live and work.*

As I regularly evaluate troubled children, I investigate their knowledge of their parents. Routinely I ask, "What kind of job does your father [or mother] do?" A few young people know vaguely the company for whom their parents work, but it is extremely rare that one can tell me anything specific about those jobs.

Since work consumes a large amount of time and energy for people, this leaves a significant gap in family intimacy. If your children do not know about your professional or work life, I strongly urge you to begin to share information with them.

Around the dinner table or while sharing other activities, talk about something that happened during your day. Yes, I know some jobs are a bit routine or even monotonous, but if you start thinking about events, I suspect every parent could spot some humorous, frustrating, or thought-provoking happenings.

Find a way to talk about such things (or even discuss your boredom!) as often as you can. Such conversations can be focused on trying to befriend or help a fellow worker. You can encourage in your children the awareness of how vital it is to develop a healthy sense of responsibility by the ideas you discuss. And you can help them develop a spirit of gratitude for your hard work, and even your sacrifices, in making a living for them.

When America was more rural or small-town in its life-style, each child knew automatically what the parents did. My father plowed the fields, tended the livestock, cut the grain, and fixed the machinery on the farm. I often accompanied him and even helped him. My mother cooked, mended, cleaned, and helped with the garden and farmyard chores. We all worked together.

When each person, however, goes off in divergent paths and meets only for short times now and then, it is easy to forget to talk. When work has been hard, and people difficult to get along with, you may prefer to forget work and not discuss it at all. Or you may find it easy to talk only about the negatives and therefore turn off your children or spouse so they don't want to hear it!

Try to avoid focusing only on the problems, but do share those as well as the happier, or even funny, episodes. It is likely that you will find your job goes better when you talk about it more. In relating the happenings of the day, you will relieve some of your tension and may even think of some improvements in the ways you cope with work.

It is certain that, as you share this essential part of your lives, your children will understand you better, are likely to respect and appreciate you more, and your relationship will be more intimate. Hopefully, your children will also learn some of the practical lessons of making a living successfully.

Education Through Training and Discipline

Eddie looked slyly at me out of black eyes sparkling with energy. Just how would I react to his mischievous behavior? He had worn out three teachers and his mother's attention was focused on him most of the time at home. Eddie had, indeed, lots of attention, but most of it was bad since he was in almost constant motion, rarely completed his school assignments, and picked on other children at every opportunity. None of his well-trained, experienced teachers could find a method of discipline that would motivate this bright child or change his behavior.

To Eddie's surprise, I ignored his messy, incomplete math

paper and asked him instead about his home life. Did he have any sisters or brothers? How did they get along? And did things go okay with his parents?

From the replies I received, I knew I needed to talk with Eddie's mother, and a few days later she gladly came for a conference. She was a woman of great strength and inner beauty, but she was heavily overburdened both on her job and at home. As we talked, she realized that she often carried home the frustrations of her work and unknowingly was displacing them on her energetic and mischievous children. She had drifted a long way from the excellent, simple parenting skills of her mother!

Eddie's mother assured me that she would remedy the disciplining methods that were so hurtful to him, but I felt I needed to follow up to be really sure. He was too special a child to risk further damage.

Two weeks later, Eddie's mother was back in the school office with me. The excitement on her face told me there was good news. Her story is one I wish I could reproduce on videotape for every parent to see!

After thinking for several days about how she could get Eddie to cooperate, his mother finally knew what to do. One day after work, she took off her shoes, propped up her feet, and relaxed in a big armchair. She turned on the TV to the evening news and opened the newspaper.

In only a few minutes she heard her son enter the room and knew he was curious about her new behavior. Why wasn't Mom in the kitchen preparing dinner so he could get to his ball game?

Without turning her head, Eddie's mother calmly announced, "Eddie, there'll be no dinner or ball game tonight until your room is cleaned and your homework done!" She watched him out of the corner of her eye as she continued to "read" the paper.

After a few seconds of amazed silence, Eddie responded, "What'd you say, Mama?" Mother gently but clearly repeated her words while looking at the news. "No dinner, no ball game, Mama?" Eddie repeated.

"No, Eddie!"

In only a short time, Eddie's room was clean as it rarely had been, and he was busily completing his arithmetic assignment. He ate a hasty dinner and just made it to the game in time.

Eddie's teachers later verified the total change in his habits. In only two weeks he had become a model student (well, nearly!), and he continued to do well throughout the semester.

Educating a child takes time, energy, and tenacity. But it also takes remembering what it was that taught you, as a child, the basic lessons that have helped you succeed. And let me remind you, it takes creativity to make these lessons really work for your child!

—5—
PLAYING
AND
WORKING
TOGETHER

Dr. Nicholas Stinnett has studied more than three thousand healthy families. He has discovered a number of characteristics that these families feel have helped make them strong. In his article with K. Sauer in "Relationship Characteristics of Strong Families," (*Family Perspective*, 1977, Vol. II), he has written about his discoveries, but one of the top six on the list is that of families sharing activities.

Enduring, happy families work and play *together!*

Working as a Team

"I just can't get Judy to keep her room clean! I don't expect anything else of her, and it seems like at least she could pick up her own room!" Judy's mother was angry but her face also registered hurt and almost despair. She wanted Judy to do well in school so she kept her household duties to a minimum.

As I talked further with this mother, I learned just how fragmented their family was. The father worked hard both on his job and at home, but he worked alone. It annoyed him to have his son try to help him because the lad talked a great deal and in his boyish awkwardness often created more trouble than he offered help.

Mother also was employed outside the home and she had developed a streamlined system for getting her housework done. She too found that Judy's "help" often slowed her down.

While each member of this family avowedly loved the others, each was becoming more and more isolated from the family. Their loving relationship found little or no opportunity for expression. A great deal of love, therefore, was being wasted.

As I worked with this busy but lonely family I remembered my own childhood. I cannot recall any task within my family that needed to be done alone. From housecleaning to gardening to farm work, we were a team. I'll admit, I often felt angry to have to stop reading or playing in order to work. In that regard I was like every child I know.

By the end of the day (or the job), however, there was inevitably a sense of satisfaction and even pride in the completed task. The love and appreciation from my parents made me feel really important. And there was always the fun and teasing from my mischievous brother and good-humored father to make even the most difficult task fun.

A fringe benefit of working together as a team is that of teaching children how to plan a job and complete it efficiently. Having grown up in a family that worked together well, I took for granted that that sort of effort just happened.

On one occasion I sent two of our children to clean up the basement. They were, I felt, old enough at eight and twelve to do that simple job promptly while I prepared dinner. When I went to check on them, I found both children busy, but the room looked far worse than it had before they started!

As I watched the two of them struggling, I realized the problem was mine! I had failed to really show them how to work. Dinner was forgotten as I set to work with them. We divided the jobs and put them in order, so one was not trying in vain to dust as the other was busily stirring up more dust with the broom. Soon the task was completed and the three of us finished dinner together.

That evening reminded me that one must not assume children know certain truths just because we, the parents, know. Knowledge is not inherited—it must be taught. And teaching children how to plan and complete tasks, how to work together, and how to have fun with one another while doing so, is one of the basic duties—and joys—of parents.

While I'm certain I didn't always feel it at the time, my memories of family work projects are those of great love, happiness, and satisfaction.

I hope you, like Judy's family, will think about your priorities in relationships. It's far more important to work more slowly, to practice patience, and to share jobs, than it is to get the work done promptly—alone. Sharing work can build a relationship.

Playing Together

While it's great to laugh together as you work, it is also important to laugh together while you play. Sound silly? Believe me, it's necessary advice.

Paul. He and his parents were not getting along—not at all! At fourteen, his long, unwashed hair and careless attire drew angry, disapproving glances from his father as they sat in electric silence in my office. For most of Paul's childhood his life had been quite separate from his father's. This man was a hardworking, success-oriented officer in a large corporation. He realized that he had not really known his child, soon to be in high school. He was anxious to mend (or actually build) a relationship with his only son.

He was striving to talk with his son with minimal success. He bought a number of expensive toys and sporting items. There was little appreciation. In desperation, he decided to teach his son to join him in golf—his own favorite sport. He purchased expensive new golf clubs, insisted that Paul join him, and off they went to the club. He patiently instructed Paul in holding the clubs, the essentials of selecting the proper one, and how to follow through in the swing.

But Paul was not really very coordinated. Furthermore, he wasn't at all sure he wanted to play golf, and he was quite afraid of trying to please this stranger-turned-father. Paul did not learn quickly and was reluctant to try very hard. It was not long before this troubled father was yelling angrily at his clumsy son. "Why can't you at least try?" he accused. "How can you be so dumb?" Paul's father, a perfectionist, was defeating himself at the most important challenge he had ever faced—winning the love of his son.

Paul's father had not learned to play for fun. He had forgotten how to laugh. He failed to remember his own youth and only focused on the serious need to win, to develop perfect style, to be proper.

While it is important to do well and even to win in both work and play, being perfect can become an elusive demon that drives you relentlessly. Such a drive will most likely destroy the very relationship you most want to develop. Just as Paul's father did, you may lose far more than a game in the end.

Sharing Activities at Various Ages

Early childhood is the time to begin playing together, just as it is the time to teach the satisfaction of working together. So, if your children are little, try to remember what you liked (as well as the things you dreaded) when you were small. Chances are, your child will share many of those feelings. You can count on a growing sense of warmth as you help your child understand how to work and as you rediscover how to play in a truly enjoyable manner.

As your child grows older, you will have an easier time recalling those delightful times of your early years. Adapt those ideas to your child's unique style in your own way. Soon you will be enjoying healthy laughter, and satisfying memories will begin to collect.

Knowing that my father played leapfrog and my mother had reveled in hide-the-thimble somehow gave those simple games status. Any game that was still going strong after all those years had to have great and enduring qualities. I know now that my parents' fun at playing those games with us related to their memories just as surely as their delight created mine!

With adolescence there arrives a new and immense challenge. In that impossible no-man's-land, neither parent nor adolescent knows from hour to hour whether he is an adult or a child. Again let me remind you, parents, that recalling your own teenage years will help. That help is even more certain if you can recapture the emotions you endured. Remembering your anguished defeats, red-faced embarrassments, and peaks of elation can enable you to offer the empathy to your young person that will heal those hurts and promise hope for the future.

In adolescence you will not have as much time with that son or daughter as you may have had earlier. But if you join in your children's school and church activities when that is possible, they will know you really care about them. During these tumultuous years, remember to consider your teenager more and more your friend and less your child.

Balances in Sharing Activities

In every aspect of life about which we know anything, we see the necessity of establishing balances. The more successful you become at finding this harmony, the more delightful your relationships will become. Consider these areas as examples of finding such balances:

1. *Humor and seriousness.* While it is great fun to laugh at work and play, there are times when it's necessary to be serious. I loved the twinkle in my father's brown eyes and the pleasure it predicted. And I knew with equal certainty that a sober look or flash of anger meant I'd better take this matter (whatever it was) seriously. My father's balance made biblical wisdom factual to me. "I will instruct thee and teach thee in the way which thou shalt go: I will guide thee with mine eye" (Psalms 32:8).

2. *Work and play.* While play is the spice that makes life palatable, work is the substance of the nutrients that sustain us. Being able to show achievements creates a sense of self-worth and usefulness in the world in which we live. A world that had become weary of materialism in the decades of the fifties and sixties has begun in the seventies and eighties to reevaluate the satisfying characteristics of achievement.

Help your children find this balance and both you and they will enjoy all of your relationships more.

3. *Responsibility and freedom.* Without a healthy sense of what he should do, and the thrill of pride when that thing is done well, no child can really value freedom. This concept is especially valid for children in elementary school. So many parents crave a carefree childhood for their youngsters! They wait on these children, entertain them, and carefully expect little if anything from them except their so-called best in school. With the finest of intentions, such parents deprive their children of the character-strengthening development of sound responsibility. And they create a dependent relationship that keeps their children immature.

4. *Dependency and independence.* The ultimate goal of every child is to become an adult with a positive identity who can make a living and can live independently. Yet every human being (admit it or not) has a need for help, sooner or later, from someone. It is the finely tuned balance between the

courage to admit a need and ask for help, and the good sense to be able to handle stress alone, when necessary, that makes life more or less successful.

5. *Grief and joy.* In all relationships there are experiences of loss with the resultant grief that must be healed. There are, fortunately, times of joy and elation that need to be shared. An intimate relationship learns to suffer the pain of shared sorrow and relish the joy of great exuberance with equal readiness. Modeling this for your children can enable them to learn to live through their own joys and sorrows with courage and dignity.

No matter what the issue in your life, you can find its antithesis and carefully establish your own balance around that concern.

It is ultimately your task to find and understand the various aspects of your own personality and balance them. The creativity in you needs to be balanced with responsibility if it is to find useful expression. Your intellect is priceless, but unless it is tempered with the richness of emotions, it becomes cold and boring. When emotions, on the other hand, are not controlled with good judgment, they can become downright dangerous. Being nurturing and protective are excellent and loving qualities in any relationship, but if they are not balanced by positive criticism and gentle nudges toward self-reliance, that relationship will inevitably get painfully out of balance.

The better you know yourself, the more balanced and harmonious you can become. The more balanced you are internally, the better friend, child, or parent you can become.

I hope you will discover and develop the delightful quality of playfulness and use it both at work and play. Have fun completing necessary tasks and revel in the sense of accomplishment you deserve. Certainly, developing skills in your play can temporarily become work—but don't forget that the aim of play and leisure is to recreate your energy and renew your spirit, so that you can again achieve whatever needs doing. This cycle of filling and expending is vital to your own life as well as that of your child, and in your relationship with each other.

—6—
LEARN THE WHEN AND HOW OF RELINQUISHMENT

It is paradoxical to think of relinquishing your child in considering relationships. Yet the ability to let go of a child is precisely what is necessary if your parent-child relationship is to survive.

In April 1981, my mother-in-law died, and I had the distinct honor of being by her side as she released this life for a far better one. Having been unconscious from a stroke for some days, she was totally unable to communicate her awareness of my presence, but I had a strange sense that she knew and was grateful for my being there.

Whether or not she knew and felt my silent good-bye, I was left with a profound new thought as I returned home alone. I was now one of the senior generation. I had no living relative of an older generation. I was it. Once I became accustomed to the significance of that status, I have rather enjoyed it. I can now tell my grandson, "Now when I was a child about your age, I heard one of the first radio programs in my neighborhood."

There are a number of dramatic passageways in life, but I believe there are only two major turning points in parent-child relationships. Each is painful in its way, but absolutely necessary for long-term health in the contacts between child and parent.

Child to Adolescent Point

Brian. He was almost through with high school. An excellent athlete and a young man of really rare integrity, he was both loved and respected by his numerous friends. He had, however, been born with a slight birth defect—unnoted by anyone but his parents.

Janet, his mother, had focused a great deal of time and energy on seeing physicians and getting the best of care to correct this mild problem. Through this excessive focus on a little problem, mother and son had unwittingly set up a major relationship difficulty.

On the one hand, Brian felt he needed Mom's supervision of his physical ailments. But she had extended her attention to his entire life. His bright eyes blazed as he described the way she acted when riding with him at the steering wheel. He described feeling furious when she demanded unfair curfews, and he often found excuses to skip meals because she even measured, needlessly, how much and how well he ate!

He was angry with his overprotective mother because she was afraid to release him. She had become so accustomed to his needing her that she feared when he no longer had to lean on her, they would drift apart until this much-loved son would be beyond her reach.

As often happens, it was Brian's youthful insight that understood his mother's overreaction. When they could finally break through their anger and discuss the issues logically, they both learned to relate differently; Mother gradually relinquished her protective role; they became friends.

I can certainly identify with Janet because I, too, hated to have my children grow up and leave me. An incident with my daughter Kathy pointed up the fact that she was growing up and I was having difficulty letting go. But only when I did let go could I find that new and even more delightful friend-to-friend relationship.

During those stormy times of adolescence, with their attendant emergence of independence, we parents commonly panic. In many cases, such panic is warranted, as young people rebel into independence instead of being carefully guided and invited into it. In our panic we do, unconsciously, precisely what Janet and I did—revert to earlier methods which once worked. All too often, when they no longer are successful, we try harder and harder, but even the most intense of such efforts are doomed to fail.

The transition of childhood to adolescence is difficult at best. But it will be infinitely more enjoyable and less worrisome when parents understand and respond to the need to steadily back off and let that young person manage his or her life with increasing independence—entering the new world of adulthood with confidence and courage.

In my own case, my despair over any major mother-daughter dilemma quietly subsided as I began to perceive a dim light at the end of my long, dark tunnel. If I were to work at making friends with another woman, how would I go about it?

1. I would need to sincerely like and respect her. With Kathy, that was not difficult.

2. I would find time to spend with her. That, too, I had already accomplished.

3. I would know that she was my equal, and as such, I would share my experiences, feelings, dreams, and my very self with her. That was where I had fallen short. I had wanted to keep Kathy as my little girl and had been, unconsciously, treating her like a four-year-old.

4. I would respect my friend enough that I would not dominate or attempt to control her. That means when we were together, we would enjoy sharing deeply with one another, but when we were apart, I would trust her to manage her life well. I know that friends call on one another for help, fun, and simply the joy of discovering and sharing life together.

Thus Janet and I turned very significant corners in our lives. We clearly made commitments to our children-turned-adults that we would treat them like adults as much as possible. You may be certain that I, at least, did so imperfectly, and often I fell into old habits. Occasionally, my daughter was gracious enough to admit that she, too, at times acted in some pretty childish ways.

As I learned, however, to see the exciting emergence of a brand-new adult in my child, I realized the risk and fear, the pain and anger, were worthwhile. And as I increasingly trusted our basic love for each other and her growing good judgment and common sense, I knew I could release her safely.

With each of my children, there has been a unique mode and different time for their release. In every case I have felt that wrenching pain of letting go of the dear child he and she had been. But as in the pain of birth itself, the new adult who came forth became my very dear friend.

Adult to Senior Citizen Point

The major focus of this book is on the relationship of parents with children. But all parents have their own parents with whom they must relate as well. I have found that many problems between children and parents are concerned with unresolved conflicts with that older generation.

Sometimes those conflicts are due to the failure of those older parents to have let go of *their* children years ago. And when that is the case, remedying the problem is most difficult. Since we get quite set in our ways as we grow older, going back and remembering, then relinquishing, is unlikely to happen.

If that is your predicament, however, do not despair. You as the adult child have the power of choice. You can use that power to stay psychologically and even emotionally enmeshed with your older parents. Or you may choose to love, respect, and help your older parents, but become free of their control. Let me give you an example:

Gloria. She was troubled as she listened to her brother-in-law and his sister arguing with their elderly father. He was in quite bad health with heart trouble, eyes that no longer saw clearly, and increasing deafness. He definitely needed medical care, and it was certainly affordable. This grandfather, however, had a stubborn streak and was determined to avoid "those doctors" at all costs. His children were pleading with him to let them help him get good medical care. After so many years, these caring adults still felt as if they were the little children of this stubborn man.

Waiting for the best time, Gloria finally intruded into that conversation. In a kind but determined voice, she outlined a plan for her father-in-law's care that was easy to follow. To even her amazement, the elderly gentleman promptly agreed. Gloria was able to function as a caring parent to him and that was just what he needed.

As an adult child you have not only the right, but sooner or later, the real need to release yourself from the child role with

your older parents. Strangely, being free from unreasonable dom-
ination can enable you to be more loving, wiser, and stronger with
them. As they age, like it or not, they will need your wisdom and
strength.

Not only will this healthy separation save you immeasurable frustration and hurt, it will enable your children to be free.
When there are power struggles and pain between their parents
and grandparents (just as is true of father-mother struggles), the
children will inevitably take sides. Since they usually have their
own difficulties with their parents, they tend to take sides with the
grandparents, further estranging them from you.

In letting go of children, I trust you understand I am not recom-
mending a true termination of your relationship. I am describing
the fact that the nature of that relationship must change. The old
protective, nurturing aspects of parenting young children must go
if your children are to mature into healthy, independent adults.

With its painful passing, however, will be born a new and
exciting friendship that can grow infinitely. How you cope with
that change determines the success of your child's transition to
adulthood.

A similar pattern is certain to emerge in your relationship with
your parents. In giving up the role of "child" to your older parents, you will assume some new responsibilities. These may feel
burdensome, but I know you will join me in discovering that that
burden is balanced by your awareness of a new strength and dignity. I trust you will enjoy this, even though you may often want
to return to the "old" days.

Returning Point

For many years I found immense pleasure and peace from returning to my old farm home. Even after my parents died, I would
drive there and bask in the warm memories of my childhood
years.

The inevitable happened, of course, and that dear, old farm
home was torn down to make space for a new, brick house. As I
sat in the driveway of the little country church nearby, I wept as I
mourned the loss of that house. To where, now, could I return for
my anchor spot in a hectic life?

And then I remembered that the relationships I had formed

were with the people who lived there, not with the house itself. It was only a symbol of our love. So I now know that what we return to are *relationships*.

As our children grow up, they become our friends if we know how to bring that about. As our parents age, we must assume a reversal of our child roles and learn to "parent" them. And finally, the ultimate release of death will occur.

When we have made our relationships ones of trust, respect, and love, we will often be distant from each other. Whether near or far by miles, however, or even when separated by death, I hope you will often return to your related one. Return by correspondence, telephone, or in memories. Such returning will enrich you both and will immortalize that relationship.

There are many ways of characterizing relationships.

In their book *Dear Dawn, Dear Dad,* John Dobbert and his daughter Dawn explore the parent-child relationship and believe the soundness of theirs is based on the three *R*s:

Recognize—We recognize the fact that differences are a normal and expected part of every relationship.

Reconcile—We work to reconcile those emotionally charged differences which possess the potential to wreck our relationship. Compromise from both parties is usually necessary in this process.

Respect—We've learned to value and respect those differences which may bother us but seem to be an indelible part of the other party's life. Tolerance, bathed in love, often changes potential problems to appreciation.

I just hope you have found some new insights through these aspects with which I have lived for so many years and that your own relationships with your children and parents will be truly blessed.

PART II

HOW TO BUILD
A HEALTHY RELATIONSHIP

During World War II, I was in high school and college. I will never forget the intensity of the emotions of those days. There was great fear of the Nazi ideology and the atrocities it created. There was deep-seated anger at the arrogant cruelty of those aggressors. We became elated over Allied victories and knew despair at the losses. The undercurrents of patriotism moved all of us and we teenagers became worshipers of uniformed men.

In the midst of these global tragedies and profound feelings, there were unprecedented numbers of hastily consummated marriages. From these marriages there were born many children whose early, most impressionable years were spent in the most insecure of circumstances. They were moved from one armed forces base to another, as young couples desperately sought to collect time and memories that might have to be enough for a lifetime. Many children were left with anxious grandparents as young mothers followed their husbands.

Besides the long separations due to fathers' tours of duty in the service, a vast number of women went to work. They sought jobs to support themselves and their babies, but equally significant was the patriotism that drove them to work in defense plants to manufacture the ammunition and equipment that could help win the war.

After what seemed an eternity the war was won. Many men did not return, and their children never knew them. A great many did come home, deeply changed by the horrors of war, to wives who also had changed. There was a massive shift in sexual mores and morality in general, and the sacredness of marriage vows was sadly desecrated.

It was inevitable, then, that a great many marriages failed. Having begun a trend, they continued to fail. It was small wonder that people fell into a frantic search for pleasure and material gain after the loss and grief of those war years. A relentless increase in divorce, hedonism, and amorality still mounts some forty years after.

The babies born in those war years are now middle-aged, and

their babies are young adults. All too many have grown up without the security and balance of their own two parents. Instead they came to know the trauma and grief of divorces and the confusion of remarriages.

This may seem a lengthy dissertation, but I hope you understand from it the immensity of the attack those events launched on family strength. The resultant destruction of security created a fear which in many families has frozen the natural expression of feelings so essential to good relationships. Healthy intimacy between parents as well as between parents and children is increasingly difficult to find. These are the facts that make it necessary to teach people how to form warm, healthy, lasting parent-child relationships.

Furthermore, even those of us who had secure and loving parents find their examples challenged by changing times. What my mother did seemed wrong to me, so I often went to opposite extremes which were, in turn, equally mistaken. There are as yet no good training schools or college courses in parenting. Here are some gleanings from my many years of experience as a pediatrician and child-and-family psychiatrist, but best of all, from my own experiences as a child, a mother, and a grandmother.

–7–
ACQUIRE THE BUILDING SKILLS

Since there has been a prolonged and profound dearth of stable marriages and families, let me describe some basic guidelines for creating your very own.

Due to the changes of the past four or five decades, we must think of families in a new manner. No longer do we find many of the classic "Leave It to Beaver" situations where moms, dads, and two or three youngsters live happily in a comfortable home in a well-kept neighborhood.

Instead, there are many families living in large cities in crowded apartments. Others are managed heroically by a single parent, or tired grandparents who are starting over to raise grandchildren.

There is no single blueprint, then, that can fit the many different life-styles to which today's families must adjust. There are, nonetheless, some basic guidelines that you parents may adapt in building your own relationships.

First, You Need a Blueprint

I have already described my own errors in avoiding my mother's tendency to lecture and scold. By my commitment to never yell at my children, I ended up being too easy on them at times or ineffectively nagging in other situations.

The father I described earlier, by contrast, identified with his father and as a result he overpunished his children, prompting fear and rebellion in them.

If you are like either example, and you don't know how to be different, look around you. Observe other parents and critically evaluate the results of their relationships with their children. As you see them being too harsh or rigid, you will detect the fear or rebellion this elicits in the eyes as well as the behavior of their youngsters. On the other hand, you will find parents giving in to spoiled offspring who dominate and control them in that destructive role reversal so common in today's Western society.

Keep looking! Don't settle for these ill-conceived categories of parent-child relationships. Go to playgrounds, schools, or sports events, or to church. In each varied setting you will discover new aspects of parenting that will be good, mediocre, or downright destructive. As you observe, you are likely to find a growing sense of rightness or wrongness that will be your clue to those modes of functioning that feel just right for you. Try those out. Discuss your ideas with your spouse or a trusted friend. As you adapt those methods to your own personality and family system, you will find a growing repertoire of skills for building a healthy relationship.

Another source for finding good role models is television. In spite of the usually misguided programming of these times, there are occasional glimpses of really great parenting—situations in which parents stay loving, while holding firmly to good values and fair rules. The use of humor to get across a needed point is not hard to find and is a saving grace in any relationship.

Some examples of excellent TV programs depicting healthy parent-child relationships include the "Cosby Show," "The Waltons," and "Little House on the Prairie." "Sesame Street" and "Mr. Rogers' Neighborhood" are excellent shows for children. By taking time to watch these with your children, you will find many opportunities to discuss ideas that will bind you together in moments of shared happiness and intimacy.

The less constructive and downright harmful shows are equally plentiful! The daily "soaps" that make light of immorality of the most damaging sorts are seen by many children and adults alike. The blatant permission to adopt such life-styles cannot be overlooked—and this applies to parents as well as children!

Books and tapes by Dr. James Dobson are widely known and well used. *How to Really Love Your Child* by Dr. Ross Campbell, and several books by Larry Christenson are only a few examples of fine books that discuss good concepts and techniques for parenting.

In reading, I have an interesting suggestion (but one which requires work!). Find a concordance and with its help make a study of biblical teachings about parent-child relationships. If you will gain a broad perspective of such time-tested concepts, you may be surprised at their usefulness. I find that the best of modern psychiatric teachings are validated by those references to timeless wisdom.

Biblical references that are great to review for starters are Deuteronomy and Proverbs in the Old Testament. Ephesians 6:4 and Colossians 3:21 in the New Testament make quite clear the attitudes that prompt healthy relationships between fathers and their children.

Needed: A Strong Foundation

It is extremely difficult to understand and truly love others until we really know and accept ourselves. In the great Commandment of Christ, that is just what I understand Him to say: "You shall love your neighbor as yourself" (Matthew 22:39).

Unresolved Conflicts. Working intensively with the problems of many families, I have come to comprehend that commandment. When there are unresolved conflicts between a parent and any of his or her near-relatives, sooner or later that old hurt and resentment will rebound. If your child resembles or acts like that person who has troubled you, there will come a time when your old hurts will unconsciously focus on the child. Without intending to, or perhaps without even knowing that you have, you are likely to displace on your child the instinct to get even with or to withdraw from that other person.

Lori. Let me explain this fact through an example: Lori was confined to bed at age fourteen due to a serious illness. It had progressed gradually, making her feel tired and listless for several weeks. As she lay there, anxious about her health, knowing very little about its seriousness, but sensing her parents' concern, her idolized older brother walked into her room. He, too, had been seriously ill as a teenager, and Lori had sat by him in rapt silence as he sketched magic with his pencil or paints. Lori always admired and adored this special brother.

She could hardly believe her ears, therefore, when he angrily berated her for being sick. If she weren't so lazy, she'd be out helping with the work. She needn't think she had him fooled, even though her parents were taken in by her act. In a moment, Lori's idol had crumbled at her feet. For years afterward his unfair and untrue accusations haunted her, marring their relationship.

Many years later, Lori give birth to a son. He was eagerly anticipated and deeply loved. As a baby and preschooler he brought little but joy to his parents. As he grew, however, he developed certain physical traits and even mannerisms that were increasingly like Lori's brother. She was unaware at first of becoming cross with her son, when those similarities surfaced, until her entire relationship with this loved only son suffered grave damage. She was unconsciously reliving the hurt feelings toward her brother that she had suffered so long ago.

Fortunately, Lori finally realized that the true source of her frustration was not her son but her brother. She was glad, as an adult, to work out those old childish hurts. Her brother was truly sorry for his rudeness, and the apology he made healed their relationship. Best of all, Lori no longer felt the anger and resentment for her son because she learned to separate the past from the present. Had her brother not been so willing to work out those old problems with her, of course, Lori could have done so within her own mind and emotions.

Parents, Accept Yourselves. This is important in building a strong foundation. Yet there are many parents who have constant, major battles with their children over traits they see in those youngsters that they simply can't stand in themselves. One mother I know does not tolerate tears since they are a sign of weakness to her. When her daughter cries, she scolds her, and they end with a yelling match. As a matter of fact, this mother really is so tender-hearted that if she let herself, she could cry very easily. Long ago she learned to cover her tender feelings with a harsh exterior. Therefore her daughter's tears threaten her protective shell, and she simply will not tolerate them.

How important it is, then, for such parents to learn to accept themselves just as they are in order to accept their children unconditionally. Here are some practical guidelines to help you do exactly that:

1. *Try to remember when, early in your life, you did feel good about yourself and what made it possible for you to feel that way.*

2. *Next, consider who or what spoiled all those good, comfortable feelings.* Usually it is a person with much authority in our lives, such as a parent, teacher, or older sibling. In my experience those people unconsciously damage the child's very spirit by harshness or even abuse, leaving him helpless, broken, and feeling gravely inadequate.

3. *As your memory focuses on experiences and people, use your adult intelligence to try to understand why they treated you in such a way.* Often it had to do with *their* problems, not you. Open your mind to consider that they may have been mistaken in their evaluation of a problem or their methods of handling it. Perhaps they were neglected or abused as children, so they were behaving as they were taught.

4. *When you think you understand them well, forgive them for those painful experiences.*

5. *Next, honestly evaluate your own past behaviors.* It may be that you were punished unjustly for things you did not do. Forgive those unfair adults anyway. Chances are, like most of us, you did some pretty bad things and deserved some punishment! Maybe you rebelled and denied your misdeed, or on the other hand, perhaps you have carried false guilt all your life. In either event, you need an emotional housecleaning.

If you have denied doing wrong, look clearly at the facts—even if you must face the ugliness of real guilt. Only when you admit your wrongdoing can you learn from it and improve. In facing yourself squarely, you may discover the need to make restitution or make some apologies. Do it, and then figure out why you did that wrong. Most of the time such misdeeds are done for understandable reasons that relate to deep personal needs. Plan, even now, how you can benefit from meeting those needs in a successful way.

If you have tormented yourself for years with false guilt based on faulty judgments, do yourself a favor. Simply let go of it. As you see the problems of those adults who hurt you, hopefully you can believe the wrongs were theirs, not yours. So go through the process of forgiving them.

6. *Practice healthy self-acceptance by listing all the positive qualities about yourself.* Don't worry about becoming egotistical at this point—just explore, evaluate, and enjoy those good aspects. Look carefully at your weaknesses and faults. Consider how you can improve, and precisely what you need to help you do that.

If there are problems you cannot solve even with the best of help and the most honest efforts, you will need to simply accept those things and live with them.

7. *Finally, avoid the extreme of self-worship or becoming an egomaniac.* If you will consider all the forces that impacted your life to give and develop those special traits in you, you will feel a profound sense of gratitude, and even joy. Relatives, friends, teachers, God Himself—all enter into the chain of benefactors that encircles successful lives.

Above all, don't give up. Searching for a healthy personal identity and acceptance is no easy task. Its rewards, however, are priceless in your personal joy in living, and, ultimately, in your relationships.

Also Required: A Solid Frame

Roberta. Her brown eyes flashed and her childish voice grew harsh as she told me her all-too-common predicament. Her parents were divorced, and she was living with her mom and stepdad. Roberta did not get along with her mother and angrily resented her stepfather. He simply wasn't like her own father, whom she really wished back. The problem that especially upset her on this occasion was her mother's often-repeated words, "Roberta, when you get upset you sound exactly like your father!" All too often she was compared with her dad, and somehow it always sounded bad! She wanted to be like both of her parents, and—ever so much—*she wanted that to be good.*

Too often, even in families that have not felt the anguish of divorce, parents blame each other for many problems. Such divisiveness causes anxiety in your children for fear you *will* separate and even more for fear they, too, have those negative qualities you dislike in each other.

Instead of blame and criticism, then, practice being complimentary and supportive of each other as mother and father. When you see your child doing something like your spouse, you can then discuss it with warmth and praise. As your child sees the good in each of you, he is likely to copy it and become even better. What a lovely basis for a glowing and happy relationship!

Keep Your Perspective

It is easy to focus on one or two undesirable traits in your child and fail to see the many positive qualities about him or her. In trying to be that good or even perfect parent, proved by having a perfect child, you may overlook the strengths and focus on the faults in your child. You may be quite certain this will not only spoil but will also destroy your love relationship. Children, like adults, can stand only so much criticism. If there is not equal acceptance and praise to balance it, your child will rebel in anger or withdraw in passive defeat. Either response will shut you out.

Garry and Caroline Clark Myers, founders of *Highlights* magazine, had this to say on the subject of perspective in their book *Your Child and You:*

> The chief objective is to maintain a perspective, to hold to proper values, to plan and think of everything in terms of its effect upon your child's future days and weeks, months and years. Keep your eyes upon him as you want him to be three, five, or ten years from now. When a problem arises, make your decision and plan your procedure in terms of his future habits and ideals. Perhaps the problem will not loom so large if you think in terms of five years from now.

In today's permissive Western culture, I see some parents who carry to an opposite extreme the tendency to be critical. They find fault with their children at explosive moments, but if anyone else points out potential or real problems, such parents rush to the rescue. In front of others, they seem to believe that their child is never at fault and by their misguided protection, they unwittingly give that child permission to continue those bad habits. Tragically, this confusing type of parent-child relationship is also doomed to failure! The children of such inconsistent parents feel highly insecure, though they often cover that insecurity with a bullyish exterior. They are afraid to live in a world where they are more powerful than their parents and they certainly do not respect them. They manipulate their parents with a "poor me" attitude when they get in trouble, and can put on an act of great pleasure—for a moment—when they get their way. But they smirk behind their parents' backs in a way that says, "Gee! I got by with it again! What a dummy Mom [or Dad] is!" This is not a good relationship at all.

By learning to step back a short distance mentally, you can easily take stock. If, for the most part, your child shows respect and compassion for others; if he or she does most things reasonably well, be grateful and proud. And let him know it. Continue to help that child improve in the weak areas, but be assured he'll make it!

If, on the other hand, you see your child in trouble with teachers, friends, and relatives, I urge you to take a careful look at him. Children who are generally disliked, who are rude and show no feeling for the hurts of others—even when they are the ones who inflicted that pain—are in for serious trouble, now as well as when they grow up.

Recently I worked with a fourteen-year-old boy. He was still hurting from the divorce of his parents but would not share that pain. He was, in fact, running from it into a wild-party cycle. He drank every weekend to the point of being drunk. When I probed to see if I could penetrate the shell to the real person underneath, I was saddened to hear him answer repeatedy, "It's no big deal!" Alcoholism, lawbreaking, cheating, lying—all had become quite okay with him. His parents had missed both trees and forest—and, sadly, the price is heavy! Be watchful so you do not lose your perspective—keep the overview clear.

I hope you can find the courage to explore your weaknesses, the honesty to face them, and the will to correct them. I know, in God's ultimate power, you can!

Allow Enough Time

Not only does it take time to build, test, and strengthen a relationship with your child but it also requires a mature builder. As the parent, you are the one who by years and experience is the more mature person in this relationship. Yet many parents I know are unaware of, or simply lacking in, that quality. There are many definitions of maturity, but the one I like best is this: "Maturity is the ability to postpone present pleasure for future good."

The mature parent is willing to be inconvenienced—gladly and lovingly—by the tiny baby's demands for feeding, changing, and cuddling. She is willing to postpone her shopping trips, her reading, or even her career if her child's needs demand it. She will become involved in her preschooler's play and her grade-schooler's activities; and he will forego his favorite TV sports in order to attend back-to-school night with his teenager.

In no other aspect of life is maturity so essential as it is in the parent-child relationship.

–8–
USE ONLY QUALITY MATERIALS

A friend of mine recently moved into an expensive new house. Less than three months after the family moved into that long-awaited home, large cracks began to appear in the basement walls. The materials used were faulty.

The same principle holds true in relationship building. Faulty information, misguided expectations, and confused understanding create the conditions that result in destructive reactions to life situations.

The Child and Great Expectations

Children and parents themselves are the basic raw materials used in relationship building. We have already discussed the importance of parents' accepting and understanding themselves and making peace with their extended families. Now we need to consider the parental expectations of the child.

All children are born with their own unique capabilities. Some are more generously endowed, and others are more limited. Even the most handicapped of babies, however, have the capacity of eliciting tenderness and protection from people.

Faulty relationship building is based not so much on the child's gifts or lack of them as on the parents' interpretation of and reaction to the child. Parents who wanted a girl and get a boy may become utterly disappointed and spoil their relationship with that son forever. If parents expect a child to be academically brilliant or a sports star, and instead have a child who is afflicted with a learning disorder, or who is awkward and small, they may feel cheated, and their disappointment can create a climate of defeat for the child as well as for their relationship.

Mistaken expectations are an almost universal problem between parents and children. The habits of the parents' own families and their childhood experiences become the unconscious patterns for their new family and their own children.

Sally. She was a young woman with whom I worked some years ago. She was only in her teens and yet she was expecting a child. The baby's father had abandoned her, and she was struggling heroically to deal with the immense anger and deep pain that were part of the grief she experienced. Tears would run down her cheeks as she recounted the many losses of her young life. She had lost dear friends through family moves, had realized that her parents had never been really proud of her, and truly felt she was worthless and unlovable.

One day Sally's father came to see me with his daughter. His disappointment in her was evident at once, and he often appeared quite angry with her. (This was obviously part of his own grief.) One of his comments was a peephole for me to glimpse a universal problem of parents. He described some of Sally's failings related to her difficulty in organizing her responsibilities and then erupted with, "Sally's seventeen years old and she doesn't even know how to clean the house! You'd think at her age she'd at least know that much!"

Quietly I asked if he or her mother had worked with Sally or required her to develop a sense of responsibility as a child. "No!" he replied irritably, "but her mother is a fine housekeeper and by her age she should be able to be of some good around the house!"

You see, this father, unknowingly, expected his daughter to absorb by some mysterious osmosis the skills of her mother. Yet he remembered, when I asked, that his own parents had painfully (truly) trained and disciplined him in that learning-to-work process. As a busy adult he had forgotten what is required to learn to work.

There are as many unreasonable expectations laid on helpless children and teenagers as there are parents. Such mistaken ideas even permeate relationships with older parents and their adult children. It is out of such mistaken expectations, then, that parents develop the painful disappointments that leave their children feeling unworthy. From their hurts, these children react in unconscious retaliation that further concerns their parents, who then increase their pressure on the child—and so the vicious cycle is set rolling. I hope you can see the inevitable destructiveness such silent misconceptions can inflict.

In constructing a building, it is basic to success that each type of nail and the different kinds of wood, metal, and finishes be used in their proper places. Shingle nails will not hold floor boards in place, and soft wood cannot be used as supports for a heavy roof.

It is exactly so with children. When parents try to make an artistic, sensitive child into an aggressive sports hero, they will weaken the structure, not only of their relationship but also of the child's entire life.

Guidelines for Using Available Raw Materials. Here are some practical guidelines for understanding how to use the raw materials of information, insight, and acceptance in building a relationship with your child:

1. *Remember your child is not just an extension of you.* He or she is a brand-new human being, unique and individually endowed with invaluable potential. Accept him or her *as is.*

2. *Explore with your child that divinely imparted potential, and find every possible means of encouraging its growth and developing its excellence.*

3. *Remember to see your child as a whole person*—not just an intellect or a physique. A favorite Scripture of mine says of Jesus Christ, "And Jesus increased in wisdom and stature, and in favour with God and man" (Luke 2:52). When you can create an environment that allows such total and balanced growth for your children (and yourselves) you will have the best possible chance of knowing a truly rewarding relationship.

4. *Just as you unconditionally accept your child, you also need to teach that child to develop the ability to respect your values and needs.* If he or she cannot become the type of person you dreamed of, at least they can respect and share the values you hold dear.

The Need for Good Counsel

At some point in erecting a building, every responsible builder seeks advice. Perhaps the soil is too soft or rocky, or the drainage is poor. It may be the pitch of the roof is wrong for the climate. Wise builders do not believe they are experts in every area of construction or that they must know it all.

Wise parents also understand the occasional need for consultation. They seek opinions from each other, friends, relatives, the children themselves, or professional counselors. At several points in my son's youth he had academic problems. I tried encouragement, punishment, and downright nagging, all to no avail. I remembered that my sister had taught school for many years, so I asked her advice.

Out of the wisdom accumulated over years of teaching experience, she reminded me that children can "burn out" when their entire time is focused on studies. She suggested that my son needed more of me and less of my discipline—our relationship had become unbalanced and we were learning to resent each other more than to love and enjoy one another. That bit of advice became something of a turning point in my attitude, and in our relationship.

In seeking to be good parents, many people fall into the habit of trying to figure out every problem and its perfect solution by themselves. They may even seek counsel from others as I did. But they frequently fail to realize that answers very commonly lie within the mind and heart of the child herself. They simply do not consider asking her what is wrong or what he needs to remedy a situation.

Nancy. A friend recently confided that her daughter's teacher had called her regarding a negative attitude that was just becoming apparent in the child. My friend went through a list of stresses that could have influenced that poor attitude, but none of her ideas seemed to fit. Wisely, she found the time to sit and discuss the issue with Nancy. As is so often the case, when parents ask sincerely and listen carefully for the answer, the solution was apparent. Nancy had observed what she considered partiality by her teacher toward some other students. The child felt this to be unfair, but she didn't know she could have gone to the teacher or even her mother for comfort or help. Remember, many children learn early to try to be independent, so they won't come to you. You must go to them.

Don't forget that much insight can be gained through the wisdom of others. So many adults I know do not read very much and they fail to watch educational TV programs or to seek out lectures and workshops on parenting. Yet most communities offer a variety of resources that can enhance your skills or reassure you about your efforts. Let me remind you, however, to be discerning about what you take into your mind. Many new ideas and suggestions are excellent, but some are mistaken and can be downright dangerous. Discuss ideas with friends or your clergyman. Ask God for His eternal wisdom to guide you about distinguishing real truth from current fads.

Faith a Requirement

Few buildings would ever be started were it not for the faith of the workmen. They have seen other buildings erected and most of them have completed previous structures. True enough, these workmen have made some mistakes that resulted in difficulties about their projects in the past. But they didn't give up.

Parent's Basic Good Intentions. In relationships, too, all of us make mistakes. And we must find the faith to remember that at the time we (or "they") did the very best we knew how to do. The thing to remember is to correct the mistake, learn to do better the next time, and then go on. Faith in ourselves, then, becomes a most important building material.

Children's Basic Goodwill. With each of my children I have had to face, in retrospect, some grievous errors. As I came to this awareness, I have sought the opportunity to explain why I made those mistakes. (The "why" was almost always a loving, caring fact!) Then I sought their understanding and forgiveness. To do this demanded faith in our basically loving relationship and in their graciousness. That faith paid great dividends in strengthening our trust and respect for each other.

Instinct. There are many times that parents actually get trapped in their own inner confusion. By trying too hard to empathize and be fair, they actually become permissive and spoil their child. At the other extreme, some try so hard to be consistent and authoritative, and end up causing rebellion against what has become rigidity. Such parents usually have lost touch with their intuition. That God-given quality called *instinct* is present in every living creature. Yet human beings lose that priceless gift by failing to understand and draw upon it. I hope you will discover and cultivate that quality in relating with your child.

God's Resources. My parents were not so privileged to study psychology or child-guidance techniques. Yet, as I now review their philosophy and most of their practices, I marvel at the soundness of their parenting skills. Those skills were based on generations of God-fearing people who taught them the practical values of living daily according to the wisdom of the Bible. It was not a book to carry to church on Sundays or to display on a table, but a reference to draw upon every day. It was their guidebook, and it worked well.

If you come from a background that did not benefit from wise and loving interpretation of the Bible and did not exemplify those practical values, you may need further help. The role modeling of less-than-godly parents and grandparents will leave you confused and wondering which way to go. Or you may pick a single verse such as "Spare the rod and spoil the child" (Proverbs 13:24, paraphrase), and use it out of context to justify serious abuse. Seek counsel from godly friends or ask God to give you His special wisdom, and then heed it.

Ask Jesus Christ. When I need special guidance in a critical time and may not be able to seek counsel or research ideas, I call on Jesus Christ. I try to imagine Him with me as He was with people some two thousand years ago. I describe my needs to Him, share my feelings, and clearly ask for guidance. Then I quietly wait for His answer as I would a human friend's. He always gives me ideas, reassurance, and precisely the responses that provide the solutions. Be very careful to do this through the power of His Spirit. He will never lead you astray.

—9—
BUILDING
DEMANDS
HARD WORK

It has become the rule in our Western culture to seek convenience. The easy, quick method for doing nearly anything seems the best. In some situations, that is true—I often use frozen foods or household cleaning devices that make housekeeping much less tiresome and demanding.

Such a philosophy, however, does not apply to building a relationship with your child. That demands top priority, constant attention, and loving determination.

The Discipline of Priorities and Time Allotment

For the tenth time during our game of Clue, the telephone rang. Dutifully I left my children and heard from a mother symptoms of the current epidemic of strep throat. After hearing her out, giving her careful instructions, and calling in a prescription, I returned to the game. The children had been patient, but this was one interruption too many! Angrily, but understandably, Wendy asked, "Mother, who's more important? Your patients or us kids?"

The answer was impossible since I knew they were my first love and concern but I also realized, as they could not, that I had an ethical and legal obligation to my patients. I know every working parent, moms and dads alike, share a similar dilemma—how to correlate the emotions in the heart with the external demands of business and other people.

Relationships are not built of negative actions or attitudes. The development of the maturity that is so vital to good parenting enabled me and others to postpone—gladly—our pleasures for the present good of our children. It is through this willing self-denial, postponement, and hard work that healthy parent-child relationships are built.

"Explore Rather than Expect"

A maxim that has become distilled for me through the stresses of my life is this: "Explore rather than expect." This means that in every aspect of my relationships, I check things out. I try to avoid looking only at a current behavior or to respond instantly to the emotion of the moment. I have learned that there is *always* a deeper layer—a core to any issue that must be probed if I am to react to another in a positive, healing manner.

Like so many other working mothers, my own answer was to deny some of my personal wishes and try to dedicate free time to enjoying my children and the mothering in which I truly delighted. Mothers who do this without the air of being a martyr find that their children don't feel like a burden. There is no underlying reluctance (which is immediately spotted by the delicate sensitivity of children). My children knew I reveled in their company, so most of the time they tolerated the interruptions and our relationship grew.

Sometimes it takes a real effort, but mothers can restrict their working hours or outside activities and phone calls. Families may choose to sacrifice materially in order to have time and energy for one another. Maybe it would be easier to stay at home, read a book, and shoo the children away. But think of the joy we would miss—times that could never be relived: school plays and sporting events; science fairs and holiday parties, plus scouting and other after-school activities. Explore what is really best for you and your children.

Cindy. Recently I had an unusual opportunity to practice my "exploring" philosophy. I was called to see a third-grade child in a public school because she was creating havoc in her classroom. Cindy could settle down and study only when the teacher stood over her and became intense in her attitude. When I visited with Cindy's mother I began to understand her problems.

This basically loving mother lived with great stress. She worked very hard in a job that carried with it much frustration and few daily rewards. Her marriage was not very loving, and her husband offered little help in the care of their three children. Due to her lack of time and energy, the quality of her time with the children suffered, and she found herself screaming at them and even punishing them so severely she later felt guilty. Due to that guilt, she would often relent and excuse them from the harsh restrictions she had imposed. They often tested her rules and found they could sometimes get by without obeying her. It was this system that set the habits which were so difficult to cope with in the classroom. The teacher could not match the energy of the mother's angry yelling, and the child's habit of testing out authority created an ongoing battle between them.

In exploring these problems with Cindy's mother, we discovered some remarkable assets with which she and I worked to make some positive changes. First, she truly understood that she was allowing her personal stress to overwhelm her. Furthermore, she knew how to avoid that—she simply had forgotten to practice her own well-established rules about leaving her work stress at the office. She decided to try a new approach to get some help from her husband. And she really understood the predicament she had unwittingly set up by being too angry with her children.

Best of all, this fortunate mother recalled her own childhood. While she knew her family had been poor and in many ways deprived, they had a mother who was a rare gem. Her mother was unusually clear thinking, fair, and loving in her parenting practices. It was heartwarming to see and hear this beautiful but tired mom describing her own mother. She recalled the calm but unbending firmness of her mother's discipline and how secure she had felt in that predictable environment. Together we formulated a plan for revolutionizing her home and family.

Many times I have helped parents work out such programs for change, but never have I seen one parent make that plan work so quickly or as well as this mother did. Only a few weeks later we met again, and I fully expected to hear that it wasn't working, and we'd have to try something else.

Instead, I saw a woman who looked serene and sounded so different I was incredulous. She told me how effectively she had transformed her attitude and even some relationships at work. In the time that had elapsed, she had needed to see her physician. Instead of her usual tension and shyness, she had felt confident and remembered to ask what she wanted to know.

Her face lit up the most, however, as she related her transformed parenting. Rather than yelling or nagging at her daughter, she sat down and began to read a magazine. Firmly she announced, "Cindy, we won't be going shopping until you get your homework done!" Frankly, Mother wasn't at all sure this approach would work, but she certainly needed to do something new.

Out of the corner of her eye, she watched Cindy, who stopped playing and after a short pause asked, "No shopping?" Mother knew the plan would work and she replied, "That's right, dear. No shopping till the work is done!" Her eyes danced as she described the prompt attention Cindy gave to that schoolwork.

Smart exploring will discover what's wrong and create a program for positive change. Such good changes will not only solve the problems but also they will transform relationships. You, too, can enjoy such healthy differences.

Keep a Positive Attitude

There is a sequel to my motto "Explore rather than expect." It is this: "When you must have expectations, make them positive." By looking for the worst possible interpretations or happenings, we can actually make those negatives materialize.

Melissa. Her big blue eyes sparkled, her cupid's bow mouth was bent into laughter, as she gleefully spooned sugar into her little brother's waiting mouth. She accidentally spilled one spoonful, and her baby brother giggled. Melissa, age three, was so excited to have made him laugh that she repeated the spill, and a new game was created—one spoonful for Bill and one for fun!

When their mother appeared, she found sticky, gritty grains of sugar widespread over the children, the floor, and the kitchen table—not a very happy way to start the day. Instead of seeing the innocent origin of the mess and understanding the children's fun, she experienced only the pain to herself of cleaning it all up. She scolded and spanked Melissa and sent her, weeping, to her room.

Fifteen years later, Melissa and Mother were still at odds. Their relationship was a pattern born of this early childhood experience—Melissa loved to laugh and was always able to create just enough mischief to be fun. But the fun was chronically spoiled by her mother's irritation. And Mother's life was a series of disappointments over her daughter, who failed to become the demure, helpful child she had dreamed of having.

Now let me quickly say that I do not think a child should be allowed to throw sugar all over the kitchen, or that she should be patted on the head for creating such a mess. I do believe, however, that if Mom had waited a moment she could have quickly understood that Melissa's intent was to entertain her baby brother and have fun herself, not to inconvenience her mom.

She might then have said, "Melissa, you're a wonderful big sister! See how Billy loves you? Now how about using this soft rubber toy to throw around instead of sugar! You didn't realize it, but sugar is a real mess to clean up. It's for eating in little bits, not for gulping and playing with. Can you remember that? And now will you help me clean it up?"

Such a postive approach sets the necessary limits, and at the same time builds a loving, respectful relationship.

Find the Balance in Intimacy and Individuality

Janelle. A cold autumn wind whistled outside my office window. Its mournful sound seemed an echo of the grief I was sharing with Janelle and her mother. For a number of months their once-carefree relationship had become more tense and frustrating. Janelle was now in her early teens and acutely aware of her mother's distress over her job, her older daughter, and other worries. Somehow Janelle (as many children do) had assumed the role of supporter and almost parent to her mom. She had become so sensitive to this woman's moods that it was almost as if she herself was feeling them. Her worry became so intense that she actually became physically ill from the stress of it. Her mother, in turn, repaid Janelle by worrying over her illnesses and concerns. The two had grown so intermeshed that neither recognized anymore whose a given problem actually was. They were too intimate.

Such an excessively close relationship is deceptive. The ability to feel what someone else is experiencing seems intimate and caring. But the danger lies in that kind of caring dragging both persons into the hopelessness of despair. Neither one can maintain the objectivity that is needed to find the solutions.

Steve. For contrast, consider Steve and his father. At ten, Steve was struggling to conquer basic math. A bright boy, cooperative, hardworking, he was much like his dad. And Dad could readily recall his own problem with math. He was tempted to pity Steve, make excuses for him, and allow him to fail. He could have identified with his son just as Janelle had with her mother. Instead, he found a tutor who knew how to correct faulty math skills from earlier years and help Steve overcome the fear of failure that blocked his progress.

Perhaps every parent has one child who is especially like him or her. Depending on how you feel about yourself and the type of habits you formed in your early years, you may either dislike certain tendencies in that child or you will overidentify with him—believing that he feels exactly as you did in a given situation. Do remember that each child is unique, a product of two parents, so only half of him came from your genes and chromosomes. And these vital substances that determine who one is came to you from all of your ancestors. So detach yourself enough to give your child that invaluable balance in knowing he is, in fact, part of you, but he is also his own unique person.

Whenever you feel that you know exactly what your child is feeling (or even thinking), discipline yourself to recall his separateness. Explore with him just what is going on and help him understand himself. In this process, you will learn to see him as he really is, a special person to be accepted and loved, but not a carbon copy of anyone.

On the other hand, some of you parents see your children at times as strangers; they are so different from you. You may even resent that differentness and feel cheated of the closeness you might have found had they been more like you. I hope you will discover the excitement of exploring this child's feelings and thoughts. Getting acquainted with such a person can be enriching and exciting, especially when it is your own child.

Letting Go Is Hard to Do

Variations in children at different ages and stages of their development presents another challenge. Just at the time you have survived the Terrible Twos and enjoyed the curious, creative threes and fours, your child inevitably turns five. Then, of course, she starts school. Suddenly she learns to love her teacher and identify with other children.

If you are wise, you will adjust to this important growth phase. You may be relieved that she can play independently or with other children. Or you may feel threatened at this big step toward independence. It is so important that you find that healthy balance in continuing to protect her and her increased self-responsibility. Watchful waiting will enable you to determine which of these your child needs. A shy, fearful child especially needs a delicate blend of protection for security, and nudging toward independence in order to grow.

About the time you have established the near-perfect balances for your schoolchild, you will find he or she is rounding another curve—this time into adolescence. Like the Terrible Twos, the Terrible Teens carry built-in challenges that will exhaust you. Starting school is the single greatest change children face. And starting adulthood is the second greatest change. The sense that the child you knew and loved so well is becoming a stranger is powerful.

Once again, let me urge you to avoid panic. Try to recall your own teenage years. Explore just who this stranger is. Careful remembering and clear-minded investigating will guide both you and him into a new, but even more enjoyable, relationship.

Make a Firm Commitment

Mark and Carol. There's one thing you don't have to worry about," affirmed Mark. "We are going to stick together no matter what!" Mark and Carol were experiencing some difficulty in their marriage. This was creating some problems with their children, and they wanted help to work it all out. Having such a firm base on which to build made working with this family a joy!

This sort of commitment is, in my experience, becoming rare. Our Western culture has given widespread permission to couples and families to work at problem relationships only to a limited extent. But when the going gets really difficult, it's all too easy to simply "opt out." It has become increasingly common for mothers to walk out on their children, and for fathers to abandon their families is even more commonplace.

There are a few situations in which tough love may demand setting some limits on what will be tolerated. In most families, however, patience, understanding and help from qualified counselors can create or restore healthy bonds. I am concerned not with just gluing together seriously fractured families, but with teaching them to lay strong foundations (or repair faulty ones) and build on those truly strong, healthy relationships.

Commitment demands maturity. The ability to see beyond the immediate moment to the future and to care about the welfare of the group more than one's own selfish interests are signs of that maturity. Be sure to step back periodically and evaluate your commitment to each person in your family, as well as to the family as a whole. It will strengthen your relationships immeasurably.

Learn Clear Communications

Relationships may be marred by many faults, but perhaps none is more prevalent than that of weakness in communication. There are enough aspects to communicating that an entire book could be devoted to that topic alone. This section just touches on the subject.

Physical Communication. Physical communication involves two facets—understanding body language and expressing feelings, especially affection, through physical means.

It is extremely important that you learn to observe the eyes, mouth, set of the jaws, posture, and gestures if you are to communicate effectively. How often have I seen a jaw and mouth set in anger or stubbornness but also detected tears in the eyes. On one occasion a patient unwittingly sat with one hand open in a plea for help, while the other was clenched into an angry fist. So often the tone of voice belies the words people say.

A gentle, reasoning interpretation of such opposites of emotion in someone with whom one is talking can clarify an issue as nothing else can. Confusion within a person and between two people comes from the mixed feelings and ambivalent beliefs within each of them. Good reading of body language can offer the breakthrough to the understanding and solutions that are needed.

The need for physical affection and comfort is universal. Quite often I work with parents whose children follow them around seeking constant attention and demanding hugs, kisses, or some sort of touch. These parents come to resent the demands of their children and even physically push them away, rather than giving the affection they crave. Almost always I discover that such parents have grown up in families that were not very demonstrative and they themselves are quite uncomfortable with physical touch.

When parents are uneasy with intimacy, either physical or emotional, the quality of their relationships will suffer. Children in such families who yearn for closeness feel rejected and try their very best to gain the parents' acceptance. The poorer the quality of the attention these children get, of course, the more they strive to gain in quantity. You can easily see what a vicious cycle this creates.

Overcoming Inhibitions. Now I believe that physical touch is instinctively needed by everyone—even those who by training have learned to block it out of their lives. So here are my suggestions to set you free from those inhibitions and enable you to demonstrate appropriate, wholesome affection to your child.

1. *Consider the kind of touching with which you are comfortable.* Perhaps you are of a teasing nature and you would enjoy a playful tweak of the ear or a bit of tickling. If so, start with such small gestures and slowly move on to a gentle goodnight hug.

Other parents may tolerate arm's length touching, so as you watch TV or read, invite your child to sit near you and stroke his hair or rub his back. Again, as you achieve comfort with this, move on to the holding on your lap or short hugs of greetings or good-byes.

2. *Keep in mind that you are the parent.* In today's world of trag-ically frequent sexual abuse of children, I respect all parents who feel a need to protect themselves from any impulse to become sexual with a child. *If you are troubled by un-wholesome thoughts about your child, seek counseling immediately.*

3. *Do not try too hard to tolerate the constant demands of an affec-tion-hungry child or seek reluctantly and against your very nature to meet those needs.* This attempt will defeat you and disappoint your child. Instead plan some special time in your day to carefully invite your child to share in a period of healthy, comfortable, parent-child affection. For preadolescent chil-dren a big rocking chair is a great place for closeness while you read, talk, or just sit quietly together. You may be more at ease sitting side by side with an occasional pat on the child's knee or arm, or perhaps with your arm about his shoulders. Just be certain to give the touches freely and lov-ingly without waiting for his demands. You will find as the quality of your spontaneous affection improves and its regu-larity can be counted on, your child will gradually stop the nagging and demanding that can be so irritating.

4. *If you continue to feel uncomfortable touching your child in any way, I urge you to seek competent counseling.* It is almost certain that some long-forgotten injuries from your past have left their scars on your emotions. Such scars can almost always be eliminated by good counsel, and you will be free to enjoy healthy physical communication as well as providing that for your child.

There have been times in my life when I and those I love have experienced immense loss with its attendant grief. It has been a miracle of healing to have a trusted person simply hold me close while I cried or rested in the security of that tangible circle of love. At other times, great joy or excitement have come to me. Again such pleasure is enhanced by the quick hug of celebration. On many occasions as a child, I felt the strong restraining touch of my father, protecting me from rebellion or danger. During most of these occasions not a word needed to be said. The sharing of feelings and experiences through such an embrace, touch, or even the gentle squeeze of a hand really says it all. I trust you will learn well the language of wholesome physical communication.

Communication Through Listening. When asked for their definition of *communication,* most people will discuss talking but few mention listening skills. Perhaps that mistake is due to a scarcity of teaching about how to hear well. In counseling families through difficulties, I find many times that one fails to hear the other because he is so intent on the comments he is going to make next that he doesn't hear her. At other times, she has been so hurt by his last accusation, she cannot focus on the thing he is saying at this time.

Here is an example of extremely good listening: During a drive with my daughter to attend a meeting, I was relating to her an event from my day. We arrived at the meeting before I could finish the story so I mentally laid it aside and, frankly, forgot it. To my amazement, as we got into the car to return home, Wendy said, "Mother, I really want to hear the rest of your story. You were just saying that you felt so excited about the meeting you had today."

Not only had my listener remembered my story but she knew exactly where to pick up on its narrative. She convinced me that she really wanted to know about my life and its happenings. That is the sort of listening that firmly cements any relationship!

The rules for good listening are easy to understand (but not always simple to follow).

1. *Stay free of defensiveness.* When you feel reasonably good about your basic intentions and motives, you can be open and honest so you will be able to hear the other person without feeling attacked—even when you are in the wrong. You will hear what is said positively so you can make needed changes, or at least empathize with the other person.

2. *Listen actively.* Active listening, touted by many today, means that you respond to the other person's statements with a look, a gesture, a question, or a related statement. You help him or her come up with some resolution of the issue in focus so that they feel satisfied.

3. *Hear with your heart.* Even the best of listeners often hear

only with their heads—their intellect. That, of course, is where good listening and understanding begins. But in my experience, many people who talk in ideas are really experiencing deep feelings. They themselves are often unaware of those emotions, but a good listener will sense the feelings and by responding to them, help that person to understand himself more clearly. It is from listening with the heart that basic intimacy is formed.

Communication Through Words. This type of communication is so logical and usual that it should perhaps go without discussion. Nevertheless, verbal communication is the poorest of all the kinds of communication. It is easy, for example, for people to hide their true feelings under a barrage of words. People who talk excessively are commonly those who are insecure, afraid of losing the attention of the listener. And most of us know people who speak with great intelligence but cover their real needs with intellectual trivia.

Another weakness in verbal communication lies in the variations in the meaning of certain words. This fact is especially evident and may be devastating in conversing with teenagers. To most adolescents, *cool* means something really great. To me, *cool* infers indifference or downright snobbery in a relationship. If you are unaware of such opposite definitions, there is no way you and your teenager can understand each other. Be certain that you ask your children to tell you the meanings of any words that don't seem to fit in your conversation.

Let me remind you that in talking (as in listening) we must speak from the heart and look for the kernels of real truth and meaning in what the child is saying. A teenager is likely to come home from school complaining, "I'm tired!" By that he may mean that he doesn't want to change clothes and mow the lawn. Or she may be saying, "I have so much homework I just can't face it." Or they may both be hinting at many other underlying causes.

In order to find out what is truly the issue, a few simple questions will help. For example, you may ask, "By that do you mean you didn't get enough sleep last night and you need a nap?" Any number of possibilities exist, and if you know your teenager, you may come up with a good guess. There are, of course, some risks in this plan. You must avoid accusations or disguised criticisms. You will cause more problems than clarification if you ask questions when you already have the answer, or if you talk "down" to that child in an angry or condescending manner. Being genuinely interested and sincerely helpful will pay off.

On the other hand, when you are talking to your child, observe his expression. If it doesn't "fit" what you are saying, stop and ask, "What did you hear me say? You look upset, and I didn't intend to upset you." Taking a minute of extra time can prevent most unintended hurts and misunderstandings. By practicing these techniques of clarifying, you will learn to hear accurately and speak precisely. Best of all, you will be building a strong friendship with your child.

Things to be avoided verbally are these:

• Never use words to label or condemn.

• Do not attack your child with critical words he may come to believe about himself.

• Avoid nagging or lecturing. Such comments create calluses on the eardrums—and the heart.

In *Between Parent and Child,* Dr. Haim G. Ginott observes:

When is criticism constructive and when is it destructive? Constructive criticism confines itself to pointing out how to do what has to be done, entirely omitting negative remarks about the personality of the child.

Larry, age ten, inadvertently spilled a glass of milk on the breakfast table.

MOTHER: You are old enough to know how to hold a glass! How many times have I told you to be careful!

FATHER: He can't help it—he is clumsy. He always was and he always will be.

Larry spilled five cents' worth of milk, but the caustic ridicule that followed the accident may cost much more in terms of loss of confidence. When things go wrong is not the right time to teach an offender about his personality. When things go wrong, it is best to deal only with the event, not with the person.

Words are for communicating ideas, warning of danger, encouraging in difficulty, comforting in despair, and above all else for saying, "You are special, and I love you!"

Communication Through Sharing. When my daughter Kathy and I were beginning to change our relationship from mother-child to a more friend-to-friend type, we did this through my new awareness of the need to share. Any healthy relationship must be a two-way affair if it is to last. Sharing the events of your day with your children is part of that two-way street. Add to that how you reacted to those events and how you felt about them, and you will have set the example for your children to share. It is my extensive experience that children will discuss the happenings of their lives just about as freely as their parents do.

Not only do you parents need to communicate your daily experiences but it is useful to share your early memories as well. Be careful to avoid such sharing in a manner that unfavorably compares your children to you. Don't lecture them by saying, "Now when *I* was your age . . ." Believe me, they will hear no more than that and will learn to resent you. Talking about the time when TV was new and many people didn't own one, however, is likely to prompt great interest in what it must have been like in those dark ages!

When I was a child, I was far from the exemplary person I perhaps should have been. But I did learn from those days and had fun being a bit ornery. Our parents were extremely strict, for example, about our reading material. While I appreciate their desire to protect our young minds from evil, I think they carried it too far. A neighbor gave us stacks of old issues of such magazines as *Good Housekeeping* and *The Saturday Evening Post* so we could collect pictures for a scrapbook. After we carefully clipped out pictures of flowers, food, and fashions, my sister and I quietly slipped those magazines to the barn and hid them.

On those long, warm, summer days while Mother was mending or taking a nap, my sister and I would sneak out those magazines and crawl up on a sloping shed roof, shaded by a huge honey locust tree. There we spent hours reading stories and articles that were really fine, but feeling excited—and just a bit guilty—because they were forbidden. When my children were old enough to get into some harmless mischief of their own, I told them the story of my childhood escapades. By this sharing they knew I understood them and forgave their not-so-serious misbehaviors. Knowing I had survived some imperfections, I believe, gave them hope for overcoming their own weaknesses.

Everyone needs dreams, and that is especially true in today's stressful world. I hope you parents have some you can share with your children. As you describe the yet-incomplete goals you may have, it may renew your lagging zeal to attain them. Even more, the sharing will give to your children the idea that dreaming dreams is a wonderful part of life for themselves too.

In C. S. Lewis's book *The Four Loves*, he describes the ancient Greek words for special kinds of relationships. In his inimitable style he discusses the *Agape* love of parent for child, the *Phileo* love of siblings, and the *Erotic* love of husband and wife. Then he cleverly introduces the love of friend for friend as the "Oh! You, too?" kind of relationship. It is this area of sharing discoveries, likes and dislikes, and the profound dreams and philosophies of life that is essential in good relationships.

Remember that you are vitally important to your child. Unless there are estrangements from unhealed hurts, that child will love to know all about you. And I hope you will equally enjoy sharing yourself so you and your child may take pleasure in evolving discoveries of mutually delightful facets of life.

Communication Allows for Some Secrets. Frankly, I like being able to be transparent. I try to live in such a simple fashion that I have little to hide. Thus I can reach emotional intimacy with others quickly and comfortably.

On the other hand, I recall an idea I gleaned from a tiny book by Dr. Paul Tournier called *Secrets* (John Knox Press, 1963). He suggested that one is not really mature until he can have a few areas of his life that he doesn't need to reveal to anyone. That seems to me to be profoundly true. In keeping with my philosophy about maintaining balances in life, it is just as important to have a few secrets as it is to be transparent!

Perhaps if we are deeply honest, every one of us has some area of our lives we want no one else to know about. For whatever it's worth, you have my permission to enjoy your special secret! Be certain, however, that doing so results in more good than harm. If ever you want to share it, find the right time and person with whom to reveal it in a constructive and useful manner. Good judgment will guide you in establishing your balance of secrecy and openness.

Grow Through Sharing Activities

Playing Together. My five-year-old eyes were wide with excitement. Daddy was playing a game with us—something he rarely had time to do. And what a special game! He was on his hands and knees with his head down, all covered with a blanket. Only his clasped hands stuck up over his head, and they were carefully tied together through the blanket with a string. He looked a bit like a turtle, and that was his name for this game.

The rules were simple. We children asked the "turtle" any question we liked as long as it could be answered "yes" or "no." Everyone knows, of course, that turtles can't talk, so this one would move his head up and down for a *yes* and from side to side for a *no*. Without warning, at intervals, Daddy would suddenly jump up and out of the blanket shouting, "Boo!" It was a real, live, Jack-in-the-Box game! Of course, we wanted him to continue forever, but even the best of fathers wear out, so he taught us to take turns being the turtle.

I hope my children remember my trying to recapture that game with them because it brought such fun to me. It is this type of playing together that helps relationships grow.

Participate in Each Other's Events. Not only is it essential to play together but it is equally important that parents attend the sports and other events in which their children participate. So many hurting children and adolescents in my practice tell me with tears and anger how they have felt when their parents fail to watch their performances. Very recently, a young college friend wept as she related that her parents had come some distance to her school to visit her. She was playing an important role in a school production, but her parents made plans to attend another event instead of seeing her perform. Even at her age, she craved the interest and involvement of her parents. If you would like a meaningful relationship with your children (whatever the age), showing genuine interest in their activities will certainly help create that.

Working Together. While playing and sharing activities are vital and can be fun, working together affords yet another facet of relationship building.

Many of my most meaningful memories are those of my large family's busily planting or tending to gardens, cleaning house, or doing a variety of tasks farms demand. Housecleaning demanded removing carpets, dismantling beds, mopping every corner, and meticulously wiping up every spiderweb from attic to basement. Usually we had to repaper the walls of at least one room, so it was a great deal of work over several days.

Every member of the family had tasks assigned, and most of those required teamwork. Fortunately my father's sense of humor filtered out among us all, and we often laughed and joked as we labored. I'm certain I dreaded those busy days at the time, but I recall the thrill of achievement at the end of the day, when the old house sparkled and even smelled sunshine clean. It's difficult in retrospect to recall whether it was truly more fun to play together or work in such a loving team.

Let me add that working together not only knits a tight relationship but it also teaches children to be organized and thorough. The old adages of "anything worth doing is worth doing well" and "cleanliness is next to godliness" still echo in my set of values.

Planning Special Times. Many families have told me they have a hard time getting along on a daily basis, but their vacations are periods of great warmth and fun. Understandable as that is, with the release from monotony and the stress of jobs, there is much to be learned from this truth.

If you can, plan short vacations frequently. A Saturday outing or occasional weekend away from the stress and irritation of regular life can do wonders in strengthening a temporarily faulty relationship. Such a vacation offers opportunities to teach democratic decision making about just where to go and how to save the money it will require. The anticipation and fun of planning such an outing can keep all of you thinking and focusing on the positives more than the negatives. As you become friends more than fighters through pursuing such positive goals, you may find the entire tenor of your lives is happier.

On vacations, several important differences from routine life become clear. There are new scenes and activities. There are jobs to be done in packing and moving on, or perhaps in camping, a great many tasks are involved. Yet because of a better attitude, everyone is more likely to function happily. There are new adventures around any turn in the highway and surprises around the next street corner.

Now consider how you can bring some of that attitude of cooperation and the spirit of adventure into your everyday living. By making little activities important and fun, almost any day can include some of that vacation spirit. A friend of mine once told me that at least once a week her husband would come home and say, "No matter what you're cooking for dinner, put it away. I'm going to take you and the boys out." Often it was just to a local fast-food place, but it was a surprise and a relief from her usual routine.

Vacation Guidelines. I *do* recommend some basic policies in your vacation plans in order to make this a constructive force in your relationships.

1. *As soon as your children are old enough, include their wishes and votes in your decision about the vacation you will have.*

2. *Explain (rather than dictate) the limits of time, money, and transportation that must be a part of your decision making.* Such an explanation will enable your children to understand your limits and respect your hard work in providing this trip. It will also teach them how to live within a budget of their own someday.

3. *Outline ahead of time the sort of behaviors and help you will each expect of the other.* As you tell your children what they may look for in you, you will find them more willing to comply with your requests for them.

4. *Keep ground rules few and simple but enforce them consistently.* You may need to pull the car over and wait for peace to return, but do have a plan for effective, nonviolent rule enforcement.

5. *Plan carefully for spending.* After the age of five, a special daily allowance will demonstrate your generosity and the

responsibility you expect of your children. It will avoid countless demands for the unlimited tourist bait that most stores provide during vacation times.

You will have your own additions to this list of suggestions for making your vacations a unique opportunity for building not only close relationships but a lifetime of memories as well.

Worship: An Important Building Block

Several people have studied extensively the various factors that make healthy family relationships. Among these forces is that of practicing together the values and beliefs of their particular religion. Some of you are certain to disagree with this fact because your children have rebelled against attending services or taking part in your family customs.

I find many families who are concerned about such rebelliousness. Almost without exception, it became apparent that such rebelliousness was preceded by a break in the parent-child relationship. Often such a fracture occurs in spite of the best of intentions.

Tom. One young teenager I know provides an example of this problem. Tom had felt put off by his parents' rather extreme religious practices, but after long delay, decided to make a genuine commitment of his faith in the Lord. He felt very relieved to be over his resistance and really enjoyed his new faith. A day or two after his big decision he was reading a newspaper and laughing over the comic strips. His mother, loving but misguided, chided him for such nonreligious reading. She wished he would read the Bible instead. Tom was so offended that he determined not to speak to his mother about the Bible or God for a long time. While his faith in God somehow remained intact, his relationship with his overly zealous mother was broken.

Strengthening Religious Ties. Few of you parents would go to this extent, perhaps, but consider what you may do, ever so unknowingly, that could equally break your bonds with your child. Here are some suggestions I believe will enable you to strengthen those ties through the daily practice of your religion.

1. *Become so comfortable with your own faith that you can express it naturally and unself-consciously any time.* Seeing God's handiwork in a rainbow, the bright flash of a cardinal, or the miracle of a new baby's smile can bring Him into focus for your child.

2. *Avoid preaching or lecturing about Him.* If you are exuberantly bubbling over about some special blessing, of course you should spill it. But avoid any sense of compulsion that will feel heavy and even austere. It is such an attitude that may defeat what you most wish to share.

3. *Be very careful to practice what you preach.* I have seen religious parents, ever so faithful to their church's activities, speak in a critical and even gossipy manner at home about the church. Such inconsistency can readily cause your child to lose respect for you and disrupt your relationship.

4. *Surround your regular, everyday conversation with the glow of your natural reverence and love for the heavenly Father, and you will be practicing your faith in the way that counts.* The best communication of your faith may not be in sermonizing or long, ardent prayers, but in the quietness and confidence that are our strength (Isaiah 30:15).

There are some family worship rituals that I do recommend because of my life's experiences. No matter how busy, our family gathered every day in a big circle in our living room for prayers. At times this practice was, I admit, something of a chore for me. But now I know its power. I recall those simple, practical prayers for protection, for the basic needs of a rigorous life during the stress of the Great Depression and the anguish of a World War. I knew God was deeply involved in my everyday life and I felt secure in His care, even when there was loss and grief. And there was that!

Two or more people cannot gather close to the same point without coming close to each other. And that is what I see as the value of clarifying and sharing your religious faith with your family. The closeness that is blessed and empowered by the love of God Himself is the very apex of intimacy among you, your children, and Him.

Strength in Cultural Events

Music. One of the great influences in life is that of music. What makes music good or bad and how you as parents handle that with your children can bind you together or isolate you! I have observed that the choice of music is a constant source of bickering or downright fighting in many families. Much of this estrangement could be prevented by teaching young children the best music.

Before your children are old enough to choose bad music, expose them to what you consider really good music. When I was only seven, the U.S. Marine Band stopped in our small town on a concert tour. As busy as he was, my father stopped work early and took us to hear this superb group of musicians. The local civic auditorium was packed and we had to stand in the rear. I was, of course, far too small to see over the crowd, so my father perched me on his shoulders. What a stunning experience! I can still feel the tingle of utter excitement as I saw the polished brass instruments and heard the stirring marches they played. To this day I become thrilled by the music of such a band.

That thrill, you see, was not just for the music or the sight of those instruments and handsome uniforms. It was the ecstasy of my father's nearness, his care that I should see even at the cost of his discomfort. It was the great effort he made to provide such a soul-tingling experience for me that all became interwoven in creating my present love of music. I believe parent-child relationships woven of such bright threads mold a child's values!

Many of you, I know, missed out on those early chances to guide your children's taste in music. Or perhaps you did your best and despite those efforts, your children, influenced by their friends, have become hooked on music you consider bad for them. In such a situation, as in other areas of life, remember that the destruction of your relationship will not win the battle. It will be won, however, by strengthening the bonds of your tender, tough, and protective kind of love.

How about listening to their music with them? Read the words on the albums (because most adults can't decipher the words for the noise). Without preaching, question them about the message in those words and think together about what is wrong (or right) with them. Leave some questions regarding that music unanswered. Such a puzzle will lead young people to think for themselves while your lectures and answers may turn them off.

Gentle guidance through such simple discussions carries more effective strength than all the power struggles in the world.

Art and Literature. These are cultural components of life that can be used to build relationships and teach some basic philosophies as well. Music, art, and literature fulfill a dual role in any civilization. They reflect the values and priorities of that culture while, in turn, they influence it profoundly. In today's raucous world, healthy parent-child relationships are so essential in helping our children to understand these cultural facts.

What an opportunity you parents have to teach your children to think with healthy discrimination! Learning the meaning of the depiction of bizarre and dismembered persons in some modern paintings brings sorrow and fear to me. I am sad for the artist who must feel torn and distorted in a frightening world. And I fear for the people of a world that has gone awry. Yet I find peace and safety through my faith in the God who will ultimately triumph—not only in my life, but in the world. Sharing such insights with your child can only bring the joy of mutual discoveries and profound insights—a great relationship builder.

In my city, periodically there are huge outcries against certain books being read by students. And this may well be a needed crusade since I know many public schools stock books and really dangerous publications on such subjects as witchcraft and occult practices. More and more young people take these weird and evil studies to heart and believe them to be a way of life.

Yet with my own children I have followed a different plan. Rather than censoring and discarding books that would not be my choice for them, I tried to read and discuss the books with those teenagers. Certainly I hadn't the time to keep up with the many books their quick minds consumed, but whenever possible, we critiqued the classics and the new and often shattering books they read. What an unparalleled chance to guide their value judgments and help them discern the good from the damaging concepts.

When I was a child, in our home library there were a few books that were forbidden to me. I'm still not quite certain about why this was so, but I think it was due to certain sexual teachings and pictures—all very tasteful and wholesomely done. I do know, however, that my curiosity absolutely peaked out because they were off limits. And I secretly read them all, even becoming bored by some of them. I believe this tendency is common to children. I wish my parents had read these books with me, as they did many others, and had helped me understand the mysteries of healthy sexuality instead of isolating me from it.

Reading and discussing books together is another useful tool, then, in building relationships. This also serves an extremely useful function in teaching facts of all kinds. But most important, it is an opportunity to teach your children to think and to be discerning about sound truth as opposed to the possibly fallacious ideas of the writer.

Relationships Formed Through Crises

Long ago I heard a speaker say, "It's how you show up at the showdown that counts." He was saying it is your reaction to stress and crises that reveals your true character. In few other areas of life is this truth more evident than in relationships.

Crises are not usually cataclysmic, though some major ones will hit us all. Those that wear away (or build) relationships are the small, daily hassles.

One day when I was in high school, I was ironing. Synthetic fabrics were quite new then, and I was unfamiliar with their delicacy. I had recently purchased a lovely new synthetic satin slip and I was ironing it to restore its original smooth sheen. As I set the iron down on its waiting wrinkles, I sensed something was wrong. Quickly I lifted the hot iron, and to my dismay gazed at strings of fabric connecting the iron to the edges of a gaping hole in the front of my elegant new slip.

New clothes were scarce (since I was saving every penny for college), and I was even more upset to notice my father observing my chagrin. Rather than lecturing me about my carelessness or ignorance, however, he silently grinned. Then just as quietly but humorously, he made a sweeping gesture with his hand that reminded me of the swaying strings of melted satin. For some time that motion of his hand and the twinkle in his brown eyes became our secret. I mended the slip, and no one was the wiser—except us!

Handling crises demands good judgment, and had I been a habitually careless girl, no doubt my father would have handled the matter quite differently. This small crisis, however, as you can tell from my recalling it so vividly some forty years later, became a cement in my daughter-parent relationship.

Recently a young mother consulted me for help to tell her grade-school son about his father's untimely death. She was strongly tempted to speak only in general terms and to keep her young child away from the funeral service. The adult tendency to protect children from the realities of life and death is certainly understandable, but my experience with children is extensive, and I have found them to have a remarkable toughness and resilience. I urged her to talk clearly to her child, to include him in the ceremonious grief rituals, and to help him through his own personal grief process.

In the life of your child and yourself there will appear many losses, heartaches, and disappointments. He or she will not always be the star in school events—some rarely will be; they will suffer the loss of friends as one or the other must move; grades will not always be excellent; each of you will fail in some of your ventures. It is your challenge in the trouble spots of life to find some sense and harvest some profound lessons from them. Perhaps that lesson is simple, like learning to set the temperature on an iron—or it may be that of finding strength and dignity to weather the ultimate loss of a loved one or a personal dream. Finding the courage, wisdom, and love with which to help one another through such crises is great cement for the bonding of a parent-child relationship.

Whatever your methods for building a relationship with your child, be sure of one important fact: *It is the emotional energy you expend that makes it work and creates the memories of which life is made.* Try to recall the earliest events in your life. If you can remember them at all, I am confident that you will identify strong feelings of love, excitement, fear, or even anger associated with them.

In a number of individuals, I have discovered a scarcity of memories, and coincidentally many of these people have great difficulty forming and maintaining relationships. Such families seem to be exceptionally unable to recognize or express emotions of almost any type. They may at times be angry, but they are rarely loving, warm, or excited about life. If you are one of those unfortunate people, please take action. Through observing others, by working at it, or by seeking counseling, you can learn to recognize and express the wealth of emotions the Creator intended you to enjoy.

–10–
STEPS TOWARD INTIMACY

A fellow psychiatrist, Eric Berne, has delineated in his book *Games People Play* several steps in the progression from stranger to friend to intimacy in any relationship. In determining the type of relationship you want with your child, perhaps these steps will help you.

Ritual

The first stage is that of a ritual. When you meet a stranger, there are several prescribed reactions that are expected. In the Orient, older customs demanded that the persons meeting step back, make a gracious bow, and clasp their own hands together. In the United States, we usually shake hands, make some very formal, polite comments, and move into other small talk or business.

In some relationships, people stay very formal and prescribed in their interactions—quite businesslike. Such a ritualized relationship is quite safe because people rarely recognize or express their emotions, but it is not very satisfying.

Pastiming

The next label is that of "pastiming." The most common example of pastiming socially is the interaction among parents waiting in a doctor's office. They discuss school, immunizations, the latest flu epidemic, even politics, but they seldom refer to any emotions they may experience—except their frustration at waiting!

While nearly everyone experiences pastiming in most social situations, some people never progress beyond it. Even in the supposed safety of their own families, they speak of only the most superficial and inconsequential matters. This level of relating to one another is certainly safe, but it is also dull and eventually cold. If some of the family crave a warmer relationship, the art of pastiming creates dissatisfaction and even hurt. Sometimes one or more of the family will unwittingly create arguments or some type of crisis in order to bounce the family out of such a cold rut. I hope you will not settle for such a relationship!

Some brave souls do, in fact, reach beyond that second level and find common interests. They find one of those "Oh, you too?" interests C. S. Lewis described and they decide they will play tennis, go jogging, or enjoy the latest edition of Trivial Pursuit together. Such shared activities will go far beyond pastiming in creating fun or excitement in a relationship. Some of my friends love camping, others tennis, or a variety of activities. Their entire lives focus on the enjoyment of these pursuits in their leisure time. But even with the fun of such a relationship, these people may never really know each other in the deep, true sense.

Withdrawing

The next level of intimacy is that of being able to withdraw from one another and still maintain a basically trusting relationship. Most of us have experienced seeing someone from our past after long absences. When that person has been especially close to us, we usually find ourselves feeling and acting as if we have never been apart.

In healthy parent-child relationships, there is rarely a constant, uninterrupted togetherness. In early infancy, babies start sleeping in separate rooms, playing alone for short times, or staying with grandparents or baby-sitters at intervals. This promotes the development of necessary independence in gradually increasing degrees. It helps parents to become aware that their child is not just an extension of themselves, but a unique little individual to be taught and protected, but allowed to be himself.

As children grow, their separation from the parents increases. By the age of six, children are away from parents about as many waking hours as they are with them. A loving, trusting relationship, though it involves periods of grieving over the loss of a particular stage in the child's development, tolerates this growing independence. Such withdrawal from one another's physical presence is bearable because of the strong foundation of understanding and trust between parent and child.

Time-out as Withdrawal. One more type of withdrawal must be understood in order to build a sound relationship. That is the separation that will prevent broken ties during times of frustration and misunderstanding.

A single mother shared with me her problems with the care and discipline of her children. After a long day on her feet as a nurse, she went home to hungry, tired, and often quarrelsome children. She found herself angrily yelling at them in order to stop their fights and gain some help from them.

We discussed the use of time-out rather than angry screaming or excessive punishment, and she eagerly tried that method. The next time we met, however, she excitedly told me of a new aspect of that old method of training children. She put the children in separate corners and set a timer for five minutes. Then she went to her bedroom, shut the door, and calmed her own mind and emotions for that period of time. When she returned to settle the issues with her children, she was in control and had a workable plan well organized in her mind.

Withdrawing from power struggles, extreme anger, or deep hurts can give you time to separate your emotions from your thoughts. By thinking clearly, you will be able to conceive creative ways of understanding, forgiving, and accomplishing the tasks of training and discipline while building ever-growing bonds of a loving relationship.

Ultimate Goal: Intimacy

The ultimate goal of a relationship is the achieving of emotional, intellectual, and spiritual intimacy. Many people never achieve this best of all relationships because they do not feel safe enough to be open about their feelings. They have often experienced a variety of abusive or neglectful experiences, or they discover that deep feelings or painful experiences they have shared have been turned against them. It takes only a few such experiences to cause a sensitive person to break a relationship.

Guidelines for Intimacy. In building an intimate relationship with your child, here are some rules to guide you:

1. *Never promise your child anything, or even threaten him or her, without following through.* No matter how tired you are or how much you dislike doing something you have agreed to, do it anyway. And act as if you like it! If you have threatened to apply some consequences to your child's misbehavior, be sure you follow through!

2. *If you tell your child you will not reveal a secret he has shared* (and this promise should be exceedingly rare!), be sure you keep that commitment. Many troubled children have told me they have overheard a parent discussing some very private matter of theirs with a friend or relative. Do not promise to keep a secret unless you consider this wise and then can hold to that promise.

3. *Never ridicule a child's ideas or feelings.* Nothing, not even punishment, can hurt as much as having someone you love make fun of you.

4. *Be fair and reasonable about rules and expectations of your child.* Major breaking of this policy will certainly estrange your child.

5. *Become clear about your values, needs, and feelings and share these appropriately with your children.* Ask them for specific help in response to your needs and then compliment them by expressing your appreciation.

During the years that I felt so estranged from my mother, she would often comment on the pain in her neck and back from the arthritis she suffered. In spite of my otherwise negative attitude, I was truly happy to massage her painful muscles, and for those moments could feel close to her. During these times, I could recall those early years of my life and how much I knew then that she and I loved each other.

6. *Discuss your philosophy of life as well as your dreams and hopes with your child.* In small increments and at times of specific events in your family's life, try to put together the memories of your past, the lessons you have learned, and their application to the present. It is such a perspective, told with honesty and feeling, that will teach wisdom to your child.

7. *Practice the art of understanding and accepting the ideas, behaviors, and feelings of others unconditionally.* You need not agree with all of these factors, but you must retain respect and affection for that other person, even when you disagree.

Intimacy demands having feelings, dreams, and needs that are worth sharing (and everyone has these if they only recognize that worth). It also requires *time* with people. And it demands an otherwise friendly relationship that is honest and safe enough to create trust. Without trust in one's own worth and the love of the other person, there can be no intimacy.

Be Understanding and Forgiving

No matter how sound and loving your relationship is with your children, there are certain to be times of misunderstanding and hurt feelings. How you deal with these crucial times will either make your relationship stronger or weaker.

My mother's exacting demands and intense attempts to create perfection in me often made life miserable for me. By its very contrast, therefore, her occasional episodes of patience and understanding were memorable.

My college brother's pursuits of learning were intriguing to me, and I learned a remarkable amount from his many shared experiences. His mechanical typewriter was an instrument of magic to my ten-year-old eyes. I used any and every possible opportunity to explore the neatness with which it fashioned words and sentences.

One day as I laboriously pecked out some paragraphs, my mother caught me in the act. Usually she had scolded me for such exploring, lecturing me on the probable costs of repairing what I was likely to break.

On this occasion, however, she quietly picked up her mending, settled into her rocking chair, and spoke to me gently. "Gracie," she stated, "I know you love your brother's typewriter. It's fun to see it make words that are so neat, isn't it? Just be careful not to jam the keys, will you?"

I knew perfectly well that I could damage the machine, so I quietly left it and moved on to other activities. My mother's understanding and gentle manner was far more effective than her usual harsh scoldings.

It is not just with young children that understanding and forgiving needs to take place. Adolescents, in fact, are especially likely to need this process. And, interestingly, they are occasionally the ones who are first to recognize and forgive faults in their parents.

Ned. He was feeling tormented by an unresolved conflict with his father. He had asked for a special type of jacket, and his father, who felt it to be a bit too extravagant, was delaying his answer. Ned, a handsome fourteen-year-old, confided to his mother that he could accept a *no* if he had to, but simply could not tolerate the indecision. He found himself nagging his father until the two of them were extremely upset with one another.

Ned's mother was aware of the frequent verbal battles between her son and his dad and was anxious to help both of them. She explained the father's own conflict, and how much he wanted to avoid spoiling his son, but that he also liked nice things and wanted him to have the jacket. She suggested that Ned relax, wait a bit, and even ask his heavenly Father for guidance. Then, wisely, she waited in silence.

A few days later, Ned's father related to his wife the following events: Ned had found a time to talk with him when both of them were feeling good. He explained his frustration at waiting without knowing the outcome and told his dad that he could accept the refusal of his wish. The wisdom of the boy moved that father as nothing else could have done. Their communication was so logical and understanding that a compromise was soon worked out. It was Ned in this case who was willing to forgive his father's painful delay and understand the reasons for it.

This example, by the way, also clarifies the role of one parent in kindly interpreting apparent flaws in the other. It is very easy to take sides with a teenager like Ned, still further estranging him from the other parent.

Adult children sometimes have a priceless opportunity to make peace with their elderly parents. Sadly enough, many years of their relationship may be lost in needless conflict. But even late resolutions are so much better than not achieving them at all.

Hannah. Even her erect posture and prim manners revealed the strong character in Hannah. She had been a highly critical person with rigid expectations and a rather austere manner. She was cordial but not warm to most people.

The time eventually came when Hannah could no longer live alone, and her children conferred about the best arrangements for her last years of life. One of her daughters felt compelled to invite her to live with her family. Yet, she confided, she could hardly bear the thought of living with this critical person for what could be a number of years. She entered into a period of civil war within her own mind—part of her felt this woman deserved a home with her loved ones, but part of her felt she could not endure it.

One day, when the elderly mother was visiting in this home, she told a story that totally stilled that battle. When Hannah was only two, her mother died in childbirth. She and her infant brother went to live with a relative. Years passed and her father remarried. The younger brother, potentially an asset in his father's business, went home to live with him, his new wife, and their other children.

Hannah was miserably lonely in spite of loving care from her relatives. Her occasional visits with the large family of brothers and sisters accented her isolation as the only charge of her aunt. She recalled fantasizing that she was going home to live with her father. She knew that he would be coming to visit her soon and decided that this was the time she would go back with him.

Carefully, Hannah packed her clothes and toys in a big bag and eagerly awaited her father's visit. Sure enough, he came. He was riding his big, black horse, rather than driving the buggy, but Hannah's magical thinking considered that no problem.

After a brief visit, Father began to say his good-byes and prepared to leave. Hannah eagerly announced, "Wait, Papa, I'll get my bag, 'cause I'm going home with you." Instead of his ready smile, she saw surprise on his face.

"No," he replied, "your home is here with Aunt Mary. She has no children and she wants you to live with her."

Hannah knew well her father's determined ways, but she argued, pleaded, and wept for him to take her home to her brothers and sisters. It was all to no avail, and the man became angry and walked to his horse, mounted, and started to ride away. Hannah was desperate. She followed him outside, crying and begging to go home. Deathly afraid of horses, she grasped the pawing foreleg of the huge animal.

At last her unbending father flicked her arms with his riding crop until she let go, and he coldly rode away. Hannah was only seven, but she made a life-molding decision that day. She told her daughter that she realized it did no good to cry and that she, at that tender age, made the commitment never to cry again. In order to reinforce that difficult task, she had become coldly logical and often critical. Hannah was now nearly eighty.

With a new and profound understanding of this reserved, strong woman, her children were able to forgive and love her as they never had before. Even the reluctant heart of the daughter was now able to genuinely, wholeheartedly welcome this mother into her heart as well as her home. In recounting this poignant episode, Hannah was at last able to cry again—and this time the tears brought comfort, healing, and true intimacy.

In all of God's creatures, there is an instinctive urge to get even with one who causes hurt. A baby chick pecks another, and it pecks back. A dog barks at a cat, and it will instantly hiss and let its claws strike out at the dog. A two-year-old child grabs a toy away from a playmate, and he will retaliate with a blow. A grown man may be cheated by a partner, and he will often get even by an equally dishonorable action.

The ability to recognize the baseness of such primitive instincts and transcend them is the hallmark of a healthy, mature person. As you build a loving relationship with your child, remember that you are the adult. You certainly may learn much from your child, but you have the benefit of age, experience, and (hopefully) wisdom. Use your advantage to make of your relationships—as parent or child—a work of beauty!

PART III

WHAT CAN DAMAGE A PARENT-CHILD RELATIONSHIP?

In the Introduction I described the profound change in my relationship with my mother after the birth of my sister. It is abundantly clear to me now that most of the damage to our intimacy emerged from my shock and grief over my displacement by my baby sister. My failure to be excited by her arrival and my resentment at sharing such glorious attention with her were totally unacceptable to and misunderstood by my mother. She simply could not see through my stunned and sullen exterior to the aching loneliness inside of me. So we set in motion, completely unconsciously, the vicious cycle that broke our love relationship. Knowing that has now enabled me to be reconciled to my mother even though she is no longer living. I trust this section will help prevent such a prolonged time of estrangement with your child.

–11–
INTELLECTUAL AND PSYCHOLOGICAL CAUSES

Misunderstandings and Wrong Information

It is not conscious meanness that causes most breaks in positive parent-child relationships. Instead it is likely to be faulty information and misunderstandings about the expectations and events of daily life.

Patty. When our neighbor's first child was only a toddler, her father and mother believed she should be able to sit quietly through an hour-long church service. The church they attended then did not provide a nursery and other children seemed to tolerate the lengthy service. When Patty's restlessness became too severe for her dad to tolerate, he would take her out and discipline her. Occasionally he even spanked her and eventually, she learned to make it through the service. But the severity of her father's disapproval became more general as she grew. Eventually that criticalness marred their relationship over a period of years.

Patty's father loved her and wanted her ever so badly to be a perfect child. But at that time he simply did not understand the limitations of toddlers. His lack of information was the truly imperfect issue—not his child's normal behavior.

In the earlier example of my mother and the typewriter, it was her ability to understand the irresistible desire to explore that helped her communicate effectively with me. More often than not, when I was a young, inexperienced mother, I misunderstood and temporarily broke my relationships with my children. Most broken relationships are short in duration and can be quickly mended, but when they go on too long or are too painful, repairing them becomes much more difficult.

Another common misconception of parents lies in their conviction that they must always be right in order to be respected. Please don't let that mistaken idea become your rule!

Barbara. Her brown eyes smoldered and her jaws set like steel as Barbara raged about her father. "He always has to be right," she exclaimed, "even when he's so wrong!" They frequently had disagreements based on his unyielding demands that she make straight *A*s in school. Barbara was a bright and conscientious student, but she knew she could not always make *A*s.

Later, when I talked with her father, he described to me his attitude. As he verbally portrayed his discussions with Barbara, the stubborn self-defensiveness she had described was quite clear. "But," he stated, "if I give in, she'll become so careless, she'll never be accepted to a decent college! I'm only doing it for her own good!" Gradually, however, he began to recognize his daughter's sense of his constant disapproval, and he understood her need of his *pride in her*, rather than his demands of a perfection that was truly beyond her reach. Interestingly, as he became more flexible and fair, Barbara, under so much less pressure, became even more successful.

Amy. The last common misunderstanding is the failure of most people to separate thoughts from feelings. "How did you feel," I asked, "when your nineteen-year-old daughter told you she was pregnant?" Amy's anguished and angry father promptly replied, "I felt as if she were deliberately trying to humiliate me!"

His face clearly depicted his anguish and his tone of voice revealed the anger, but his words expressed an accusing thought rather than a recognition of these powerful emotions. So the angry accusation against his daughter pierced her heart like an arrow, and in no time there was an escalating battle between them.

Only when Dad was willing to accept some guidance could he recognize what he was doing. To try to avoid his fear that he had failed as a father, he was accusing his child. And finally, when she understood her dad, she could reveal her vulnerability and how desperately she had needed to hang on to her boyfriend—even when giving in to him put her at such a risk. Her pregnancy had nothing to do with trying to hurt or humiliate her father. It had a great deal to do, however, with her profound need of his unconditional love and encouragement.

Guidelines for Clear Expression. It is usual that adults confuse "feeling" with "thinking," though feelings are implied in their ideas. It is essential to verbalize both with clarity. In considering the identity of the emotions that are so vital to maintaining a healthy relationship, here are some concise rules:

1. *Look for words such as* like *or* as if. In discussing feelings, those words are clues to their confusion with facts. "I feel sad," or "I'm very angry," are distinctly emotions. But when I hear, "I feel as if she is hurting me," I know the ideas and accusations are covering the true emotions and that a guessing game or outright battle is imminent.

2. *When you have clarified how you* really *feel—hurt, afraid, worried, angry, loving, happy—try to be precise not only about the proper word but also about how intensely you are experiencing that emotion.*

3. *Find a way to express that feeling (even if it is anger or hurt) in a clear and loving way.* This will prevent most of the defensiveness that will otherwise be generated. Remember, anger is also part of loving or caring about someone.

4. *Finally, accompany the expression of that feeling with a concise statement of what you need in connection with that feeling.* "I feel really worried about your friendship with Jim, since he does drink a lot. And I need your reassurance that you will cool it until he decides to stop that dangerous habit."

In order to ensure compliance with such needs, the most important single ingredients are basic love and respect in that parent-child relationship. Be certain that you constantly build those qualities into your lives.

Misinterpretations of Behaviors

Earlier I quoted the illustration of the child who enjoyed feeding sugar to her baby brother and then thought it hilarious to

throw more sugar on the kitchen floor. It was the mother's misin-
terpretation of that behavior which threw her into such an angry
response. She saw it as an act of foolishness at best—and downright troublemaking at worst.

Helen. There are almost as many other examples of this relationship wrecker as there are families. Helen is a friend of mine who
teaches school. After coping with teenagers all day, she returned
home one evening to find her teenage daughter and a girlfriend
entertaining boyfriends in their home. There was a strict rule
against such activities unless one of the parents was there.

Helen panicked! She knew of several teenage girls who had recently become pregnant, and one of her worst fears was that of
her own daughter facing such a predicament. She yelled as she
lectured her child, implied that she was certain to end up a prosti-
tute, and grounded her for three months.

Fortunately, this agitated mother finally regained her compo-
sure and was eventually able to talk rationally with her only
daughter. She learned that this basically careful girl had simply
been overwhelmed by her friends' insistence on stopping by her
house for Cokes and conversation. They had actually done nothing amiss and had no intentions of wrongdoing.

It was Helen's awareness of danger and her knowledge of the
ease with which teens fall prey to the temptation to explore adult
sexual activities that alarmed her—and understandably so. Her
interpretation of her own daughter's behavior, however, was entirely wrong. Furthermore, her accusations were extremely destructive. Many a young person has broken off a previously good
relationship with a parent because of such unfounded doubts. Be
sure to keep your expectations *as positive as you can, as long as possible,* while still being aware of your teen's vulnerability. Save those
lectures and heavy consequences for real, verified misconduct.

Keep alert to the tensions that develop in your own relationship
with your child and that of your spouse, as well. Those tensions
will often be your clue that the relationship itself is in danger. Interpreting your intentions, values, and communications to your
child without becoming defensive will often prevent the breaks in
that closeness you crave. It is usually easier for you to see those
misinterpretations between your spouse and a child than it is for
him or her to perceive them. Once you recognize them, you can

help make those basically loving intentions clear, the verbal misunderstandings straight, and the support system of your entire family strong.

Mistaken Identity

Ginny. Today I sat at lunch with a friend who is having serious problems relating with her adolescent daughter. As we chatted I listened carefully for those little clues that could enable me to help my friend Ginny. Those clues came loudly and clearly as she stated, "Debbie is the spitting image of my mother! She was so critical, and I could never please her, and now I feel exactly the same with my own child!"

I have heard (and written about) so many nearly identical situations that I marvel at the frequency of misidentifying a child. Sometimes it is a child's physical appearance that is remarkably similar to a relative or spouse. Even more common, however, is the constant reminder by a child's behavior or attitudes of that other person's negative impact. This stress begins in preschoolers and grows in its intensity into adulthood. Almost always the similarity, with its painful memories, is unconscious.

Through years of experience I have learned much about the problems that stem from the heartbreak of divorce. One of the most frequent issues that stem from broken relationships is that of the child who resembles the absent spouse. Most children who suffer this misfortune draw upon themselves the disapproval of the parent with whom they are left. Let me reiterate, *such disapproval is rarely conscious, but it is nonetheless devastating.*

In most cases, children of divorce love both parents and yearn for the family to be reunited. They need to complete the formation of their own individual identities by having good times with both parents, and they want the approval of each parent. Therefore, when that approval is lacking because John looks and acts like his dad, or Jill is so similar to her mom, the one parent who has been hurt by the other is very likely to resent those similarities.

The child interprets this resentment as personal rejection. Even when he or she understands this problem to be related to parental struggles, he is left with confusion. "If I can't be like Dad (or Mom), then who can I be like? How can I know how I should be?"

Believe it or not, I have actually heard children ask these exact questions.

Ginger and Kerry.   One last interpretation needs to be made. Ginger's teenage daughter was always (so it seemed) in some major difficulty. She and her mother argued almost daily, and yet they loved each other in spite of the insults they regularly exchanged. One day, Ginger called me with an insight that was to revolutionize her relationship. She had realized that her daughter had become a mirror to her of the traits she most intensely disliked in herself.

Ginger's next task was to endure the pain of realizing how much she had hurt her child because of her failure to understand such an important fact. Then she had to forgive herself, seek God's forgiveness, and learn to accept herself as His child. When she was free from that destructive self-condemnation, Ginger was ready for the next step.

With some quiet ceremoniousness, Ginger sat down with Kerry and began to explain to her the far-reaching impact of her introspective journey. She interpreted to her daughter that what had seemed to be such condemnation of her—the child—really belonged to herself—the mother. She further told her about a childhood, lived with a critical mother and a distant, cold father, that had made her grow up feeling ugly and guilty about many mistaken facts. As Kerry understood the dynamics of her mother's problem, she realized that she, too, was not so bad—not perfect, of course, but not a hopeless person either!

Almost every relationship has some areas of distress and difficulty. Interpreting one's self to another and exploring the tensions with that other can result in great insights, and such new understanding will certainly strengthen a relationship just as much as its lack weakened those bonds!

Psychological Defense Mechanisms

Whether you know it or not, almost everyone grows up using certain unconscious devices to protect them from hurt feelings. Put very simply, I am convinced that the ultimate emotional pain is that which results from a judgment by someone important to us. That judgment, stated in a variety of ways, is simply this: "You're bad! You're not okay!" The fear of rejection or abandonment is an instinctive one and it involves not only the fear of physical abandonment but also the dread of emotional exclusion. When such massive rejection does occur, children will do almost anything to get past it and to renew the warmth of acceptance.

Five Major Defenses. Several categories of defenses are certain to be marshaled in the child's (or later, the adult's) attempts to restore a harmonious relationship. We will discuss five of the major ones:

1. *Denial.* When mothers accuse a child of breaking a cherished object or eating cookies before dinner, most children will instantly deny doing so. The angrier mother sounds, the more vehemently the child will insist that he didn't do it. When a parent is conned by the child's denial, and he does avoid the dreaded punishment, the next time he will deny even more earnestly.

When people practice such a deception long enough and intensely enough, they may actually lose the capacity to know what is true. While the lie may temporarily protect the child, it is a symptom of a weak relationship, and eventually that weak area will produce a total breakdown in the trust that is so essential in a healthy relationship.

When parents or teachers come to me with concerns about dishonesty, I can predict with great accuracy that the adults have been too threatening on one hand, and too ready to believe the lies on the other hand. With equal certainty, I know the child is sensitive, and wants desperately to gain the parent's love and approval.

People who carry on this habit of denial may temporarily gain a certain relief, but they suffer long-range damage to their reliability, and eventually will lack true integrity because they can no longer clearly discern truth from lies.

2. *Projection.* When there is more than one child in a family, this defense will be clearly seen as a sequel to denial. The older child who denies breaking a vase is quite likely to

continue, "Kenny did it!" Kenny, in turn (if he can talk) will spiritedly assert that baby Linda did it, or he may even blame the pet cat.

Most parents catch on to such tricks and eventually pin down the responsibility for misbehavior, levy the consequences, and teach the necessary lessons.

For a variety of reasons, however, some parents believe the child's dishonest explanation. Perhaps the child is especially loved, and the parent needs to maintain an image of perfection. At times a parent may feel so antagonistic that he is afraid of abusing a certain child, and so he lets himself be fooled. Let's face it, some children are so convincing, it's difficult to be certain. At any rate, many children grow from childhood to old age putting the blame on anyone and everyone else. It's the teacher's fault, the boss's unfairness, the spouse's unreasonableness, the children's laziness—but never is it their own responsibility.

People who perfect this very destructive habit will damage or destroy most of their relationships, because other people don't know when they will turn on them with unfair blame.

3. *Rationalization.* This is the habit, so subtle it can catch any of us unaware, of twisting one's thoughts to conclude whatever we choose. I see this habit in many adolescents who don't like to study. As I discuss their academic weak spots, I ask them about their study habits. The usual replies are a series of excuses. "They really don't expect us to do homework," or "I do all my studies in class," or "I know I can make up all those lost assignments over the weekend," or any of dozens of such thoughts which I call wishful thinking.

Parents and children alike fall into the use of this defense to excuse themselves from effort, and yet they assume they can maintain a healthy relationship. "I know Suzy knows I love her. Why should I tell her every day?" "When Kent gets older he'll outgrow his habit of procrastinating." Parents who wish for such magic protect themselves from the hard work of disciplining themselves or their children or risking the child's temporary antagonism; but they run a far greater risk—that of seeing a child's potential wasted, and perhaps losing the respect that is so vital to a good relationship.

Most of us know people who frequently brag or dream about an exciting project or invention that they will complete tomorrow or next year. Such people somehow never quite make it to the fulfillment stage of those plans. These folks are those who have mastered the dangerous art of rationalizing—they live, ever so convincingly, in dreams that could be realized—if only they would add work to their wishes! These people are skilled at rationalizing.

4. *Displacement.* Larry worked very hard and was extremely successful, but he gained success by handling everyone with whom he worked with the proverbial kid gloves. His office staff adored him, and he was able to get a high degree of co-operation and performance from them. Yet his work was demanding and created immense stress in his life.

He could hardly wait to get home at night, therefore, so he could release the pressure of his work and be himself. Sadly, Larry's true self was critical and demanding, so the restrictions he placed on his interactions all day did not help him in those vital family relationships. In order to unload his stress, Larry was short-tempered with his wife, snapped at the children, and was even known to kick the faithful, old family dog.

Larry did exactly what many good people do—he took out on his dearly loved family the frustrations that really belonged at work. He was too insecure to be direct and honest with his employees for fear of losing their loyalty. Feeling more confident of the understanding and love of his family, he could displace those reactions more safely on them—or so he thought.

Unfortunately, as his children grew older, they became evasive and were no longer there when he came in the house. They shrank from his harshness and never found a way to understand what was really going on. It takes a truly committed and mature person to understand and accept such displacement and maintain a loving relationship. It is even more difficult for the one who has this habit to change.

5. *Reaction Formation.* Julie's transparent blue eyes looked anxiously into mine. I had been talking with her and her mother about the development of her sudden fear of the dark. She had been a "usual" sort of child until a few months previous. There were times when she fussed with her younger sister and was not always as prompt in her obedience as her mother would have liked.

Recently, however, she was the perfect child at home; at school she was exceptionally studious, and rarely took part in the competitive games of the other third-grade children. Despite such model behavior, Julie had become increasingly afraid of many things. She worried about her parents and was fearful lest they have an accident.

The worry in Julie's eyes revealed to me the need to talk privately with her. It was only when her mother returned to the waiting room that Julie overflowed with the pent-up concerns of recent weeks.

It seemed her mother, under a great deal of personal stress, had become unusually harsh and impatient. Julie felt she could never please her mom and felt angry about this new and frightening distance that was widening between her and her mother.

Believing the problem to be her failures, Julie tried harder and harder to be perfect, and when she continued to fall short, the anger she felt became complicated by fear. She was afraid that her anger at her mother would be punished by some imagined tragedy. Julie had reacted against the normal imperfections of childhood and went to extreme measures to prove her goodness.

The use of one extreme to protect oneself against the other is not at all uncommon. My vow to avoid yelling at my children was my reaction against my mother's early tendency to lecture and scold me. It protected me from my inner frustration and temptation to yell at their occasional misbehaviors.

In relationships, however, this defense eventually is destructive. My going to that opposite extreme made me seem uncaring about my children's misbehaviors, as my daughter so clearly revealed.

Julie's excessive goodness resulted in disappointment when it failed to stop her mother's irritability.

When one set of feelings or behaviors isn't working too well, I strongly urge you to try to find a happy medium where calm reason and positive attitudes can help you find solutions that will work.

Unrealistic Expectations

Every prospective parent has dreams of the children they hope to have. Those dreams relate closely to the parents' unfulfilled ambitions or, sometimes, to their desire to relive some glorious period of their lives. A father, for example, may want his son to be the football hero he once was (or yearned to be!), and a mother may wish her daughter to be at least a runner-up for the title of Homecoming Queen.

Dreams Don't Always Come True. And when they don't, it takes a wise, mature parent to accept reality. Yet I know one dad who ruined the lives of several of his daughters because he could not accept the loss of his dreams. Frank was a macho man in his day and cherished the belief that a real man must have strong, masculine sons. Instead, he had a series of seven lovely daughters and not one son. He made it subtly clear to those girls that they were inferior and were only to be tolerated—not loved and accepted. This man tragically missed out on the fun of a relationship with even one of those truly bright, fun-loving, and successful girls.

By contrast, a family whom I served as a pediatrician was faced with a total loss of their dreams of a healthy child. Their very first, long-awaited child was born with Down's syndrome. Their child was to be extremely limited in his potential for an independent life. Yet, when offered a chance to place this child in a caring institution, they refused and courageously turned from their original dreams to the challenge of reality. They tenderly loved this handicapped child, and helped him develop to the maximum the capabilities he had. They developed an especially loving relationship with their son that inspired everyone who knew them.

Perfection Is Relative. It is understandable that parents wish for achievements from their children that will bring credit to them, the parents. Many parents are even more unselfish—they want

achievements from their children that will open a number of opportunities for them. The father who wanted his daughter to make
all *A*s really wanted her to be able to attend big-name schools if
she chose to do so.

Children, however, are quite sensitive to their parents' tendencies to use their successes as excuses to brag to their adult friends.
And they are likely to feel used and therefore resentful of such
attitudes. Furthermore, these parents often fail to accept any responsibility for or share in their children's failures, though they
do take much of the credit for their successes. In either event, the
children, especially adolescents, become angry and commonly
break off their relationship (emotionally) with that parent, at least
for a time.

The problem with demanding perfection from a selfish motive
is that the child feels the parent's love is conditional. Conditional
love puts any relationship at risk and sets patterns in motion that
will negatively influence every relationship in life.

Even when perfection is demanded for the sake of the child, it
is almost certain to create discouragement within the child. Such
unrealistically high expectations are usually unreachable, either
because a child is truly incapable of them, or because perfection-
istic parents tend to constantly raise their requirements. Like the
high jumper in track and field meets, the young person in this
type of family eventually can reach no higher. He or she will
probably rebel in anger or give up in despair, and the parent-child
relationship will be damaged or broken.

A Sense of Failure for the Learning Disabled. A friend of mine has
studied and worked for years and has developed a highly successful method for working with learning-disabled people. She
has discovered that nearly one-third of those whom she has studied suffer from various degrees of learning disorders. I agree with
her observations that children who have such difficulties experience a sense of failure. They feel inferior to their classmates and
are sensitive to their parents' disappointment. The emotional
component of this widespread problem adds to the underlying
learning disorder, further increasing the failures with their devastating impact.

When parents understand this problem and encourage their
children, eventually they will compensate and discover how to
learn. On the other hand, when parents misunderstand this prob-

lem and see it as a child's laziness or stubborn refusal to try, then the child is almost certain to give up. Most important, however, is the influence of the parents' attitude on their relationship with their children. An encouraging, optimistic attitude will seal a loving relationship and give hope to the children. It is equally certain that a critical, power-struggling attitude will defeat both parents and children and break their relationship.

(For more information on this new concept in treating learning disorders, write Dr. Pat Lindamood at 1315 Morro, San Luis Obispo, California 93401.)

Learning disabilities, of course, are only one category of disappointments that can mar or break parent-child relationships. Any particular dream you may have had for your child may meet with the disillusioning fact that he or she simply will not be able to measure up. It is imperative for a healthy relationship that you accept that fact. Help your child to explore the possibilities that he does possess, and to develop them the very best that he can. Working together with love and encouragement will build the sort of real bonds between you that are far more meaningful than the best of dreams!

Confusion of Roles

In today's Western culture, social role definitions have become frustratingly fuzzy. Even the means for clarifying masculinity from femininity are extremely clouded. And the roles of parents and children are equally distorted. Both parents and children have great difficulty knowing whose responsibility are the various activities of the home. Mothers and fathers as well are commonly at odds because each feels overburdened and undersupported by the other.

Marvin and Brenda. They are a current example of the mother-father conflict. He was raised in a family in which the father earned the income while mother managed the children and the household duties. This pattern never varied through the twenty-five years Marvin lived with them.

It was Marvin's absolutely clear expectation that his wife, Brenda, would perform precisely as his mother had done. She would keep an immaculate house, raise well-mannered, successful children, and cook delectable meals daily. What Marvin failed to understand was the complication of today's economy. In order to keep up house payments and provide the niceties of life that he enjoyed, Brenda had to go to work.

Brenda had also grown up in a family where the old role definitions were the custom. She willingly and heroically tried to maintain excellence in both functions—the traditional one of being homemaker and mother, as well as the new one of career woman. Only when she found one of her children suffering from emotional problems did she realize how frustrated and overloaded she was.

Brenda had assumed dual roles while her husband stayed with his old, single function. She simply could not handle all of her responsibilities, and yet she failed to ask for help because she had not realized things could be different. She was taking out on her children the frustration she felt from her overload.

Parents need to understand one another's needs and form new "job descriptions" of parenthood for themselves. If both parents must work, then each should assume equal shares of the daily household tasks as well. Earlier we discussed the necessity of sharing work and play if family relationships are to be sound. As you learn to do such sharing in your own special way, I predict your entire family's relationships will be the better for it!

Clarifying the Roles in Your Family. Male and female roles definitely need to be clarified by each family. At one time, the culturally prescribed modes of dress, manner of walking and talking, and professional limits helped make these differences distinct and understandable. One by one, these distinguishing characteristics have been discarded by our society. I feel quite certain we cannot revive those old ways, but I'm equally positive that each of you parents can do some specific things to help reclarify these definitions for yourselves and your children. You may thereby avoid many of the disagreements and battles that spoil some relationships.

1. *Think clearly, and carefully observe others around you until you formulate your own patterns of sexual role fulfillment.* No matter what others do, you are an individual and you have the right

to determine each issue for yourself. So practice dressing, behaving, and feeling as you want to—in the manner that is comfortable for you as God's child.

2. *By your own example, show your child what you believe a good woman should be, and what you feel proud of in a real man.* By all means be careful to avoid society's false macho for men or seductive values for women, and develop within your definition the qualities of gentleness, honesty, and selflessness that are real and lasting.

3. *Verbally explain your values and instill these qualities into the minds of your children.* Compliment them when they demonstrate these traits and be sure to express your appreciation of one another as moms and dads. Be careful to avoid any concepts that even hint that all men are bad or that most women are dumb!

4. *As you read magazines and watch TV be aware of negative implications about those basic male-female roles.* Draw the attention of your children to such fallacious ideas and help them avoid falling, unknowingly, into such a belief system themselves.

5. *If your children have already developed patterns of behaving as boys and girls that are confusing or negative, discuss these habits calmly and logically.* Don't expect a so-called tomboy daughter to change overnight. A boy who is something of a sissy is not going to reverse this trend instantly—if ever. But each can add some traits or modify others so they will fit comfortably into your family's values or roles. Perhaps you will, above all else, help them discover the basic traits of being decent, caring, and thoughtful human beings. Sharing such values will add to your relationships.

As you clarify your beliefs and values and live them out in your family life, you will be strengthening your relationships—and your child's entire life, as well.

What if your child becomes a homosexual? A growing number of parents are having to face the possibility of adjusting their attitudes and thinking regarding homosexuality. While biblical injunctions are clearly against such habits, there is an increase in both boys and girls who fall into and finally choose to continue this life-style.

I have seen parents permanently break their relationship with such a young adult child. They simply would not tolerate him or her, and their angry rejection cost them all hope of a later reconciliation.

My advice to parents of such young people is to be rational. Stay loving with them and offer them counsel to make such changes as they are willing and able to make. The loneliness and confusion of the homosexuals I have known is tragic. They need love and acceptance as persons, even when you cannot accept their way of life.

Role Reversal. Another area of confusion is that of the parent-child role reversal. In today's topsy-turvy world, such dangerous changes are extremely commonplace.

Grace. When I was a child, I experienced an unforgettable masterpiece of discipline. (Parent-child relationships, by the way, are at great risk during disciplinary action.) I loved to play and read and really disliked most work when I was young, especially when I had to work by myself. So, over a period of time, I had developed a habit of forgetting certain assigned tasks.

One autumn night I had gone to bed, and carefree as I was, fell promptly to sleep. To my amazement I awakened to hear a stern voice calling my name. It was my father, and he demanded my presence in the living room. This time I didn't even need to look at his eyes to see if he meant business! This was a serious event, and he told me in clear and definite tones that I was going outside, alone and in the dark, crisp, autumn night, to do the job I knew very well needed to be done right after school.

It was my regular job to carry in kindling and wood for our old, wood-burning cookstove. Without these supplies, my mother would have difficulty preparing the big breakfasts we all enjoyed. The wood was splintery and heavy, and I did *not* like to carry it into the house and put it in the woodbox. But I knew perfectly well that I both could and should have done so earlier when it was light and warm.

In my childhood, Father's wisdom was ultimate and his authority was beyond question. My own conscience verified the timeliness of his stern discipline, and silently I obeyed, fearful of the impenetrable shadows and shivering even under my coat. There was no spanking, no lecturing, only a simple, "I want you to never forget your work again!" And back to bed I went. Let me assure you, I never did forget that job again!

Eileen. By contrast, this story reveals the reversal of parent-child roles in many families today. Eileen, fourteen, wanted to spend the night with her girlfriend. She insisted they would study together, but her parents had a valid rule that their children spend nights with friends only on weekends. She hassled them and pleaded to have her way. Finally Eileen threatened, "If you don't let me go, I will go anyway. And I won't be back!"

Only a few days previously, a teenage child of a neighbor had run away, and the anguished parents still did not know where she was. These concerned parents gave in to their strong-willed daughter and allowed her to break their good rule.

Again and again I hear such stories. Well-meaning but confused parents are abdicating their God-given responsibility. Rather than providing the basic protection of their wise, experienced authority, they find peace at all costs easier. They even allow themselves to believe that the happy excitement of a child who gets her way means they are building a loving relationship.

Nothing could be further from the truth. A child or adolescent who is more powerful than his parents is afraid, and underneath his excitement at getting his own way, experiences guilt and a loss of respect. If no one is wiser or stronger than he, what kind of a world is this? Though they do not show these vulnerable emotions, and often are not even aware of them at the time, they are actually tucked away. During times of stress, the weak character of such powerful youngsters will crumble, and they will certainly experience difficulty.

It is through wise, consistent discipline (balanced by growing freedom that rests on demonstrated responsibility) that the trust in your relationship evolves. Without that fundamental trust, no relationship will last, and weak character will be formed.

Ben. He had suffered suspension from school for the third time this semester. His teenage face was set in chronic anger and his eyes were carefully focused on the floor as we talked. Ben was intelligent, a capable student, but he usually got his way and the school officials couldn't tolerate the disruption he caused. His mother glanced at him fondly, obviously upset by Ben's anger.

She began to tease him and soon got him to laugh as she turned his serious misbehavior into minor mischief. When I asked her what she planned to institute in order to teach Ben how to behave in school, she assured me he really would be fine. He was, she said, very much like she was—enjoyed laughter and really meant nothing serious.

As I glanced at Ben I detected a fleeting look of concern, covered quickly by a stubborn glare of conquest. He had won again—but beneath the power was the bleak awareness that he was losing more and more.

Ben's mother was parenting like a child. She could quickly get her handsome son to laugh, and she herself loved to laugh and play, not to be serious and responsible as a mother needs to be.

Coconspirators. This is another type of role confusion—the parent unconsciously joins the child in misbehaving, rationalizing away the potential seriousness. She joins him in being an irresponsible child for the dubious benefit of a laugh and surface goodwill. Such child-parents may equally well lose control and scream at a child in immature, ineffectual anger. In either event, the relationship suffers, because the strength of the tough love consistency is missing. Such a relationship is immature and creates a dangerous environment for the child.

"Not as I Do . . ." One last area of confusion in parent-child relationships must be mentioned. That area is the discrepancy between the parent's stated beliefs and his demonstrated values. The father who punishes his son for dishonesty, but brags about cheating on his income tax, is the classic example of this confusion.

I once knew a mother who was extremely religious and sincerely meant to live her faith. Yet this woman was harshly critical. If the minister's concepts did not perfectly agree with her theology she would disparage his sermon throughout Sunday dinner. The love she so thoroughly believed in was not evidenced as a part of her family life. And her children became turned off by her inconsistency. Once again, a relationship not based on consistency will suffer.

Unhealthy Competition: The Family Triangle

It is quite clear to me that our society is struggling with a major misconception related to competition. For a number of decades our industrialized and urbanized culture has set the stage for a growing type of cutthroat competitiveness. The relentness surge up the corporate ladder almost proverbially depends on the damaged people who are crushed beneath the so-called winner. Many onlookers have become so disgusted at this devastation that they have come to believe all rivalry is bad.

I must say that I recognize major fallacies in most extremes and certainly there is danger in these two opposite poles! Sibling rivalry in which one child must win at the expense of another is just as destructive as the corporate ladder; but the excitement of happy competition will spur both opponents to great efforts. Out of such effort comes the growth that breeds healthy self-esteem and creates fun and respect on both sides.

While corporate climbing is a well-known entity, and undue sibling rivalry plagues many parents, I find many parents who fail to recognize their own competition with their children. Let me assure you such rivalry will destroy both your relationship and your opponent.

Chuck. He was an excellent basketball player, a rookie on a major professional team. He worked hard at practice and followed training rules religiously. After his first two seasons, therefore, he was horrified to find himself cut from the team. In great despair he sought counseling to try to discover what had gone wrong.

I reviewed Chuck's history and began to unearth some revealing material. His father was a sports coach in a good school and took great pride in his own athletic skills. When Chuck would get his dad to play with him, he struggled heroically to earn his respected father's pride in his efforts. As Chuck reminisced his way through those adolescent experiences, despite his restraints, tears flowed from saddened eyes. He could not recall even one time when his dad had expressed any approval. With increasing fervor, Chuck tried to do better and listened carefully to his dad's advice.

One fateful day, this tough older man pronounced in disgust, "Chuck, you'll *never* make it in basketball!"

Even then this talented, conscientious young man refused to give up. With each step of progress, he saw himself proving a little more that his dad was mistaken. But in the end, the powerful father's edict was correct. Chuck was washed up! He could not, indeed, make it in basketball!

In various, hidden areas of their beings, some parents feel so inadequate that they unknowingly damage their own children in their nagging need to prove themselves. I find in most such parents an interesting repeat pattern of defeat in competing with their parents. They love their children, but can't tolerate the child's eventual transcendence over them.

In the next example, you will learn how parents may compete between themselves in order to win a child's special loyalty.

Sarah. Jane, a friend of many years, phoned me one evening sounding distraught. Recognizing this as a true crisis, I invited her to come over, and soon we were sipping a comforting cup of tea as I heard her woes. Jane and her husband had only one child, a beautiful girl who had brought immense joy to their lives. In the last several weeks, however, Mother had noticed signs of some worrisome degree of rebellion. Sarah was finishing junior high and feeling really on top of the world; she no longer helped Jane about the house; she argued about every rule; and her grades were falling a bit. Sarah was quite preoccupied with boys and hardly had time for her usual church activities.

Now almost every adolescent in this country, if not the entire world, shows similar traits at this time in their lives. The difference in Jane and Sarah's story lay in yet another factor—it was the attitude of the father. Ever so gradually, he was becoming quite tolerant of Sarah's little problems. An issue of some significance had arisen when Sarah insisted on attending a party at which drugs and alcohol were to play a prominent role. Sarah, of course, believed that she could avoid these dangerous chemicals, but her mother knew only too well how her friends might function. More than one young person had experienced a first-time drug experience through a friend's "prank." Slipping something into a soft drink was thought to be funny to some of those wild youngsters.

Nevertheless, Sarah's father was holding out for the permission for her to attend. As Sarah told him how stubborn her mother was, and how much she appreciated his trust in her, this doting man totally capitulated. He had gained his daughter's surface loyalty at the price of her safety and the estrangement between Sarah and Jane. Fortunately, in this case, early counseling helped straighten out what had become, almost overnight, a dangerous family triangle in which Dad and daughter ganged up against Mom.

Unfortunately such side taking quickly becomes a vicious cycle in which Mom's strictness prompts Dad's leniency. In turn, seeing the danger of his permissiveness makes Mom all the more strict—and on it rolls.

Let me remind you to be exceedingly aware that one of the best ingredients of your own strong parent-child relationship is the loving support and encouragement of the other parent. Your child is part of both parents and needs to know positive facts and to experience warm and loving feelings for both. The parent who promotes such all-around warmth will be well loved in the final analysis.

–12–
EMOTIONAL CAUSES OF BROKEN RELATIONSHIPS

It is difficult to separate psychological from emotional influences because they are so closely interwoven. How one thinks has a major impact on the emotions, and (conversely) the way one feels often changes the way he thinks. What we will consider together in this chapter are the primary, negative, emotional factors of fear, anger, worry, and guilt. Many times these painful and damaging emotions lie undercover in what psychiatrists call *the unconscious mind.* Nevertheless they have a powerful influence on reactions to one another in a relationship.

Fears

As a child I struggled endlessly over misunderstandings with my mother. She was a good woman of great faith in God, but we did not get along very well. Because I felt so guilty about my share in our difficulties, I recall being extremely frightened when she would become ill. It seemed to me that she was ill much of the time, so I recall being frightened a great deal. Somehow it seemed I was the cause of her illness.

Because these experiences were so devastating to me, I vowed never to let my children know if I did not feel well. On one occasion I recall feeling totally exhausted after a twenty-hour stint at work without sleep. I lay down to rest before it was actually bedtime, and my little girl came to the bed to see what was wrong. I saw in her tender eyes the same worry and fear I had so often known. Heroically, I made myself get up and fake the pleasantness I was too tired to feel.

Two-way Door. While part of my heroism was a loving gift to my family, I must admit that much of it was for myself. I somehow had to compensate for a quality of life I felt I had missed. Children do understand parents' limitations, and unless those limitations are excessive they tolerate them well. I was unwittingly depriving my children of a rare chance to comfort and help me in a way that could have enhanced their self-esteem and enriched our relationship. Even in parent-child relationships, there needs to be a two-way door of giving and receiving.

Punishment. Another childhood fear is that of being punished. One young father I know was overpunished by his parents (perhaps by today's definitions, downright abused). His memories of the physical and emotional pain from his past made him react oppositely. He simply could not bring himself to discipline his children at all. Had it not been for the balancing effect of his wife's common sense, those children would have become out of control.

On the other hand, a mother with whom I worked for some time felt that her abusive parents (abusive in my opinion) had made her as successful as she felt. She decided, therefore, to apply those same abusive punishments to her children, who were becoming totally estranged from her. This mother had become so intimidated by her parents' anger that she could feel strong only when she became as angry as they were. She exemplifies some of the dynamics of child abuse—rarely done out of anger or hatred but out of an unconscious fear and sense of weakness.

Alice. She had endured a great deal of ridicule as a child. She came from an economically deprived family, and couldn't attend the events or spend money as her friends did. Alice felt horribly left out. She isolated herself and refused to join in even the activities she could have shared because she felt so inferior. Other children, not knowing why she was different, teased her, adding to her sense of loneliness and rejection.

Many years later, Alice married a man who became successful in his business, and they were quite well off materially. As commonly happens, however, her children occasionally came home from school complaining about some perfectly normal bit of teasing.

Such events caused Alice to bristle with rage. She could not see her children for who they were—quite normal, well-accepted youngsters on the whole. She saw, instead, her own remembered childish profile reflected painfully in their lives, and she would angrily respond to those teasing friends in a way intended to protect her children, but actually to protect the old helplessness and hurts from her past. Her children came to resent her interference, and their relationship with her was tarnished by embarrassment.

I hope from these examples you can see the disastrous consequences of unresolved childhood fear. On the one hand you may copy the overreactions of your parents, or you may go to the opposite extreme, making different but equally damaging mistakes. You might even build up enough emotional calluses to make you appear to be indifferent. Let me assure you this is the worst of all mistakes. A person who evidences the worst of emotions will be tolerated much better by a child than one who seems cold and withdrawn.

Anger

As I have explained earlier, the emotion of anger is nearly always a cover-up for serious hurts, worry, or even fear. Even in newborn infants, anger is evidenced by physical pain. As a baby matures, emotional pain will also result in anger. Fortunate indeed is that child whose parents understand the workings of that protective mechanism and help him, through the healing power of their love, to get over those hurts.

Chrissie. She was constantly intimidated by her father's angry demands of her. He expected instant obedience, complete with a smile, no matter what she was doing when he requested something. Now Chrissie was a bright and strong-willed child, and she simply could not bring herself to such robotlike compliance. Habitually, therefore, she would dawdle and delay just enough to see if he really meant what he demanded or if, perhaps, she could get him to be more kindly.

They lived in a perpetually malfunctioning relationship, therefore, as he continued in his angry demands and even angrier disapproval of her resistance. Chrissie, in turn, lived in fear of her dad's anger but felt compelled to maintain some of her own identity and independence. She learned to match his anger with her own, and the anger between them continues to grow because neither is yet able to recognize its source—leftover anger from Dad's childhood, and his fear that he can't be powerful enough to raise his daughter right. He feels powerful only when he is angry, and fails to realize that such anger only begets more anger and rebellion.

Just as parents' fear may find expression in two extremes, withdrawing or overreacting, so will anger result in opposite mistakes. Either it will find expression aggressively in hostile demands or explosive abuse, or it may result in icy rejection.

Natalie. She had a father who was a classic cold rejector. He was a respected man in his profession, but at home he could be unbearable. Natalie, now an adult, wept as she recalled his perfectionism and the rigidity with which he tried to enforce his often-unreasonable demands.

The man would severely spank her and then would deliberately withhold any attention from her for several days at a time. There was no discussion of her wrongdoing, and worst of all, no forgiveness. Natalie recalled going to him with tears, begging him to say it was okay, and to show her he still loved her. Somehow that stern, ice-cold heart of his refused to melt, and he would maintain absolute rejection until he felt she had suffered sufficiently. Small wonder that Natalie had major problems in her own family!

Some parents who have suffered the results of anger from their childhood learn to deny this emotion. They repress it until it suddenly explodes beyond their control, or it comes out in disguised expressions of which they are unaware.

Don. He was a comic, well loved and enjoyed by most people, but at home that humor often became sarcastic. As he related to his children, they frequently were left in tears. Later when they discussed their feelings with their mother, it became apparent that they were simply confused. Had Daddy meant the verbal jabs he gave them or was it "humor"? Mother herself was often unsure because Don had learned to disguise his hurts and anger with a form of wit.

For some years, I disguised my own anger with hurt feelings and tears. As I've discussed earlier, these two emotions (pain and anger) go together. When we deny either one we cannot express them clearly, or resolve the problems that cause them.

Carolyn. Hiding anger from oneself will almost inevitably result in its explosion over some minor thing. Carolyn knew how it felt to live with an angry father, so she carefully controlled her own anger so she would never hurt or frighten her children as he had.

When her children spilled milk she patiently wiped it up without a word. If they had problems finding shoes that matched, she searched diligently until she found the lost one. When those same children argued and fought, she gently intervened—even when she was so irritated that her eyes flashed and her body tensed.

By the end of most days, however, some small event would trigger the big explosion. Jimmy's slamming the door for the tenth time would be all it took, and Carolyn would lose control. Screaming at the startled boy, she sent him packing off to his room, wondering what in the world he had done this time.

After her explosion, Carolyn would be in tears, remorseful again for behaving just as her short-fused father had done so regularly! I'm sure you can imagine the problems both she and her children experienced in their relationship. She would often rescue Jimmy even from those disciplinary actions he deserved and needed. Jimmy, in turn, not knowing what to expect, developed nervous habits (tics) that were a symptom of his anxiety.

Guilt

In other books, I have described in detail the difference between real guilt over a known mistake or sin, and false guilt over some imagined misdeed. In parent-child relationships either kind will produce problems.

The indulgent parent (who, like Carolyn, becomes excessively angry with a child) is most likely to make a grave mistake. Since much of this emotional reaction is subconscious, people are likely to act out those feelings rather than rationally understanding and expressing them. In this confusing manner, therefore, a parent is very likely to feel guilty and try to compensate for "losing it" by rescuing or giving in to the child later on. Instead of simply apologizing for being too severe, but allowing the basic discipline to stand, the parent may spoil the whole thing by the rescue.

Tim. For example, Tim's mother knew he dawdled and repeatedly annoyed her by missing his school bus. She frequently threatened to make him walk to school the next time he failed to be ready. But each time her soft heart would win out over her clear head and she would end up taking him. The day finally came, however, when she did send him out to walk the few blocks to his school. Tim recalled feeling a sense of relief that he was, at last, paying the price for his irresponsibility. He thought, "Boy! It's cold out here! Tomorrow I'll really get up and be ready on time!" Really, he felt rather proud of himself.

He could hardly believe his ears when he heard a familiar car honk! It was that guilt-ridden mother of his (who felt she had been too harsh) who came by to take him the rest of the way to school! Tim recalls this episode as a very bad turning point in his life. He would never have to pay for his own misdeeds, because mother or someone would always do it for him. Tim's relationship with his mother was a close one, but it was hostile and overly dependent—a burden to both of them.

Guilt may be equally destructive when it is denied and hidden away. If you have ever done a rude or wrong thing to someone, you know that sense of shame that keeps you from looking that person in the eye. I know many parents and children alike who do truly hurtful things to one another and somehow do not bring themselves to apologize.

Parents mistakenly fear that any admission of wrongdoing will cause a child to lose respect for them. They simply do not understand that children intuitively know when parents are mistaken or downright wrong, and they will respect them even more for admitting that and simply saying, "I'm sorry!"

When parents are willing to own up to their mistakes, they may do an excellent job of role modeling by apologizing. When Mom and Dad can say, "I'm sorry," then children, too, will learn how to apologize. And what a loving relationship it is when both parties keep the atmosphere between them free of hurts, guilt, anger, and fear.

Ambivalence—Mixed Feelings

Sharon. She is a young woman who has taught me a great deal about the destructive force of mixed emotions. Until the age of ten, she was extremely close to her mother. She recalls that they laughed, played, worked, and occasionally wept together.

She is not certain what it was that came between them. I suspect it was Sharon's development into womanhood that worried her mother. At any rate, the mom became overprotective, watching every act of her daughter. At the slightest provocation, the mother would lecture or accuse her daughter.

After several years of such strange new attitudes, Sharon, hurt beyond expression, decided to leave home. She was able, at sixteen, to get a job, moved in with some older teens, and even continued in school for a while. Eventually, however, Sharon became immensely homesick for her mother and begged to return home. Her mother was unable to realize how she had hurt her child, believing only that she meant to protect her. Her old accusations recurred with new vigor, and Sharon was unable to tolerate the rejection she felt. On one hand she deeply loved and yearned for the mother of her past; on the other hand, she was both angry and afraid of the woman her mother had become.

In this case, Sharon discovered, finally, that her mother had suffered jealousy over the attentions her father showered on her. He certainly paid little attention to Mom. In her emotional quandary, complicated by her refusal to even admit her jealousy, this mother had resorted to secretly drinking to drown her sorrows. It was her exceptionally loving, mature daughter who discovered this fact and finally got her mother to seek the help she needed.

This is an extreme example, but perhaps it can help you to get in touch with similar mixed emotions you, too, experience. That love-hate confusion is common and perhaps to some degree is nearly universal.

Parental Immaturity

Within the past decade, I have seen increasing numbers of younger parents who have not quite grown up. Due to changes in our society, they have not completed their own childhood. These parents were allowed to stay overly dependent on their families, were not required to learn healthy responsibility, and yet they have acquired children of their own.

Such childlike parents often try to dump duties on each other.

Neither wants to get up at night with a crying child. Or if one is responsible, he or she truly gets saddled with an unfair share of family duties. Children in this kind of relationship are likely to feel that they are a burden. One depressed adolescent from such a home said, "I just wish I could die! I know my parents would be better off without me."

Child-parents usually discipline in an argumentative fashion. When I overhear them, it sounds like two siblings fighting rather than a parent teaching his child the basic lessons of life. They also enter into their children's wrongdoings, especially when they like a child and tend to see him as a "chip off the old block." Then they will let him get by with serious misdeeds. These parents tend to relive their own early experiences through their children. Thus, they are likely to give them too many things and too much money. They may even play with their children to the exclusion of teaching them the value of responsible work.

Some child-parents are so busy playing out their perpetual childhood that they parent their own children only minimally— or not at all. These carefree "adults" watch or play sports whenever they wish, they take trips at their own whims, and in general "do their own thing" with little concern for their offspring. Many school staffs discover teenagers left to their own devices for days to weeks at a time while their parents pursue their pleasures.

Such immaturity in parents does not offer answers to the needs of children, and therefore precludes a true parent-child relationship. Eventually such parents may become playmates of their children, and may even become friends of sorts. But the profound bonding of parent to child in the development of basic trust and security will not be enjoyed by such parents or their children.

Atypical Emotional Problems

There are a few special types of emotional problems that damage parent-child relationships.

Bonding. One of these is the rare failure of a child to bond with its mother at birth. Such failure to establish that instinctive, deep, and permanent bond with the mother is rare. It does occur in animals in rare instances, usually when the mother is ill.

At times I have worked with mothers who have a seemingly

normal relationship with other children; but in the case of one child, there appears to be a rejection, even from birth. Such a mother states, "I don't know what was wrong, but she would never let me cuddle her. She always felt stiff and seemed to prefer lying in her crib to letting me hold her." Eventually a mother is likely to give up and quit trying to feel close to such a baby.

As I have investigated such cases, I have found these mothers to be faced with unusual stress during their pregnancies and afterward. They are usually moderately depressed and often have too little help and encouragement during the neonatal period (the first weeks after birth). I suspect the sensitive infant feels that tired mom's tension and responds to it with the initiation of one of those vicious cycles of ever-increasing stress and seeming rejection. Even later in life, however, many such parent-child relationships can be improved if both parent and child are willing to work at doing so.

Troubled Marriage. Another disturbance in parent-child relationships comes from a troubled marital situation. When husband and wife are not getting along well, it can seem like a good idea to have a child to build a bridge between them. The fallacy in such an idea lies in the proven fact that babies are not construction engineers. They are, instead, the amorphous wet cement that demands molding in order to become set in a useful form. There are more disagreements born with babies than there are unifying effects. *So do not trust a child to mend a fractured or weak marriage.* That child is more likely to suffer than to be close to either parent.

When a marriage suffers distress after there are children in the family, every relationship is placed at risk. Unless there is serious and obvious abuse involved, the children want to remain loyal to both parents and constantly wish them back together. But hurting and unwise parents all too often set up a battle array. Each tries to look good to the children, even at the cost of putting down the other. Before long, the children in such a situation break off loyalties to both parents. They resent their parents' perpetual squabbles and they especially hate being used as spies or messengers between them.

Oftentimes, as the spouses heal from a divorce, the children are still left with divided loyalties and incompleted grief. All too often the adults involved in a divorce are hurting too much to recognize the grief and pain in the children. These children typically feel abandoned, and are unfamiliar with the process of grieving. They are left with scarred emotions and damaged family relationships.

Tempermental Differences. The work of Dr. Stella Chess and coauthors in *Temperament and Behavior* (Doubleday) reveals the last type of troubled parent-child relationship. After several decades of study, she learned that mothers and babies are often born with quite different temperaments. A mother, for example, who is quite energetic may bear a child who is unusually placid and has a low energy level. Such a discrepancy may set mother and child at odds from birth. No matter how much love there is, or even how secure the bonding between mother and child, there is very likely to develop a tense relationship. Such an energetic mom may very well feel impatient and even irritated with her slower-moving child as he (or she) grows.

It is especially important for parents to learn the gentle art of unconditional love and acceptance—even when your child is quite different from you.

Inability to Relinquish the Child

In a few families, one or both parents find it unusually difficult to let go of a child. From infancy on, they are very close to that particular child. They may even be overly protective and they tend to focus most of their interests and activities around the relationship with him or her. Despite this closeness or even because of it, there are occasional painful arguments or fights due to issues of control.

This type of parent-child bonding is exceptionally tight, and relinquishing the child is not likely to happen in a natural, progressive mode.

In my experience, such parents, themselves, have endured a series of painful separations. Many of them had parents who died or in other ways abandoned them. They cling, therefore, to their own children in order to enjoy the family closeness of which they were deprived when they were children.

When such unconscious attachments continue, a healthy adolescent begins to struggle for freedom. Just as an energetic colt who has too little space will finally jump the fences, such a young adult will instinctively, almost compulsively, break loose. And the yearning parent who so desperately needs the child's closeness will be hurt and angry at his attempts to reach normal independence.

Occasionally, out of obedience, respect, or a great sense of helplessness, a young person will not make that needed breakaway to healthy independence. When this failure happens, a physical bond will be maintained, but it is most likely that hostility will subtly invade the relationship with the development of a sick dependency. This will cause emotional pain and impose personal limitations that are unfortunate.

While intimacy between parent and child is delightful, it must be based on freedom to choose rather than be coerced. And the intimacy *will* evolve through the changes in the natural course of life into an ever richer, though different, quality.

In *Have You Hugged Your Teenager Today?* Patricia H. Rushford has these suggestions:

DEPARENT WITHOUT DEVASTATION

1. Keep telling yourself, "I can cope with anything," and "I *will* survive." These positive statements will give you reassurance. Don't forget to ask for God's help. Although there are many areas we fail when we try to do it all ourselves, with God we can make it.
2. If married, move closer to your spouse. A romantic candlelight dinner for two. Plan quiet, nonstressful times together—often.
3. If single, develop close friendships, where burden sharing is an equitable part of the relationship.
4. Build yourself up by developing outside interests. This is not a time in your life to be falling apart, but rather a time to pull yourself together.

It is painful for most parents and many children to go through this process of release. Without that relinquishment, however, each is certain to suffer an even more severe type of pain. My reassurance to you lies in personally surviving that with my own parents and children. The joys of being dear friends as well as erstwhile parents and children is well worth the pain.

Failure to Be a Place for Returning

Anne. Her soft eyes brimmed with tears and her voice broke. Anne was trying to help me understand her predicament. Her husband was having an affair with a woman at his place of business. Her four young children were a handful, and she was hurt, exhausted, and confused. I had suggested that she get her parents to look after the children for a weekend so she could get away, rest, and sort things out.

Anne's present tears were not for her wayward husband or her energetic and mischievous children. They were prompted by her acute awareness that her parents were not there for her. Many times she had sought their counsel and had asked for even a few hours of help with the children. On every occasion they had made it quite clear that they had raised their children, and it was now their turn to enjoy life. They were afraid if they gave in to her need even once, she would impose on them regularly.

Anne was abandoned—by her spouse, her friends (who felt her husband's straying was somehow her fault), and now by her parents. Her predicament reminded me of the great number of grandparents who are heroically standing by their adult children during heartbreaking crises. And by contrast, it also reinforced my painful awareness of a great number of selfish grandparents. Tragically, they have bought a bad ideology that is part of our hedonistic society. Some grandparents fail to provide that vital place for returning. The refuge, so essential for survival in the storms of our narcissistic world, is missing in many families—a sadly selfish parent-child relationship!

Conclusion

In considering parent-child relationships, it is useful to remember that most relationships suffer stress at times. They may even break under that stress, as this section explains. The best and healthiest relationships may need to take that risk at times.

Parental love must not only be tender; it must be tough as well, and at times it will endure a child's anger in order to provide him or her with the protection that is absolutely essential to his overall safety. Such a balanced parent-love will win in the long run, and will achieve a strong and enduring relationship with a child.

Unless you are willing to take that risk, however, and to cope with your child's temporary rejection, you are likely to lose your relationship permanently.

Perhaps this is part of the meaning of this profound statement of Christ: "He that findeth his life shall lose it: and he that loseth his life for my sake shall find it" (Matthew 10:39). Only that which is important enough to involve the risk of loss is worth having.

I do hope you will cultivate that rare quality of total parental love that commits you to your child forever.

PART IV

HOW TO MEND BROKEN RELATIONSHIPS

Some of the material in this section will be familiar to you because it has been discussed in earlier chapters. I hope you will use that information now to help discover how to repair any damages in your relationships. If parents have not avoided the pitfalls that lead to broken relationships, it is not too late for mending. As you read this section, examine yourself to see what did cause the breakdown in the relationship with your child. Once you've honestly determined the cause, you can set about to right the wrongs.

Due to the dramatic cultural changes taking place, I am discovering that many parents believe they are doing everything right and that problems with their children are due to faults in others—not in themselves!

Scott and Louise. These parents are clear examples of this. Their marriage has remained sound, but neither parent gets along well with their only child. He has been involved in many underhanded and a few blatantly rebellious activities. Both parents have been strict to the point of rigidity. They have all too often excluded him from their activities, and they rarely compliment him. When he does wrong, they find it difficult to forgive him, so he is left chronically in disfavor, under a cloud of disapproval.

Unfortunately, these strong-willed *parents* see their parenting as perfect. They feel that they have set limits and enforced them consistently—excellent parenting! They point to their strong, loving marriage as proof that excluding their son has been right. And they believe that their constant disapproval and stern attitudes are the very essence of the often-touted tough love.

What they fail to recognize or admit is the negative, disapproving, critical attitude that has crushed the very spirit of that only son. They are unwilling to face the need for the changes in themselves that could transform their relationship with him to one of fun and warmth! And they need not sacrifice good discipline to do that.

I hope this section will give you insight into how to change your parent-child relationship if it needs that. There is great hope for healing if you will find the courage to face your situation honestly!

–13–
TYPES
OF
RIFTS

There are two important types of rifts in all relationships. I know of not a single friendship that has not at some time suffered misunderstandings or some unavoidable breaks in even the healthiest of bonds.

Temporary

Most such problems are brief in duration, mild in their implications, and easily resolved with an even stronger relationship resulting. The lifelong friendships (usually few in number, but priceless in value) that most people have enjoyed testify to the truth of the first type of broken relationship. It is that of a temporary, easily mended kind.

The child, for example, who is angry and sullen because his mother requires him to clean his room, temporarily takes a detour away from his friendship with that parent. He wishes he never had to see her ugly face again and thinks seriously about running away from home.

When the hated task is finished, however, and his mom genuinely brags about the splendid job he has done, the anger quickly fades. He, too, really likes a neat room and is rather proud to show it off to his friends who come to play. Suddenly his mother is beautiful, and he would never think of leaving her.

Parents who are worthy of that title will gladly risk those rifts for the final payoff of rearing a confident and reliable child.

Long-Term or Permanent

The other major break in parent-child relationships is quite different. It forms slowly over a long period of time. The gap widens almost imperceptibly but relentlessly. The misunderstandings become deep hurts with a retaliation factor resulting. Such broken relationships often become lifelong battles. Many couples mistakenly believe that getting a divorce will end such struggles, whereas the opposite is often the case. The insults and counterattacks tend to become even more vicious as time goes on.

Lifelong rifts, tragically, occur in parent-child relationships all too commonly, as well as in marriages. Instead of exploring the hurts and remedying the misunderstandings, such people come to expect the worst, react to that in the most destructive ways, and set in motion a vicious cycle that may permanently force them apart. Rather than risking any further pain, such family members become coldly polite or simply totally ignore each other.

Dan. His shaggy beard and long hair matched his casual attire, which gave him a generally unkempt appearance. His face was already set at the age of twenty-two in lines that told of a fast-paced life that had vainly attempted to block out the core of pain within him. As he told me the story of his life, his voice varied from the high pitch of anger to the breaking of the sadness he had known for so long.

From the age of ten, Dan had tried in every way he knew to please his father. His dad was a coach, so Dan had gone out for basketball. He practiced shooting baskets until his hands were numb. He worked out faithfully and never missed a practice. But in spite of his most arduous efforts, Dan missed too many free throws and stumbled awkwardly when he tried to dribble the big ball down the court. He ended up on the sidelines more often than not, and when he looked at his dad, Dan saw the shame and even anger in his eyes that tormented his very spirit. After a while, Dan stopped looking at his dad. I noticed while we talked that Dan often avoided eye contact with me, as well.

After struggling through high school, Dan left home. He simply could not cope with the constant disapproval, verbal or silent, that he felt from that implacable father. To make matters worse, he found that his mother, too, seemed to dislike him. She rarely smiled at him, did not touch him, and nagged at him daily about his room, his grades, and his appearance.

For five years, this bright, capable, angry young man avoided his family. He occasionally worked as a trash collector in a large, western city, abused drugs regularly, and behaved like a bum. Only rarely did he see to it that word indirectly reached his family informing them he was alive.

Through a series of other family problems, Dan's parents finally came to realize what their rigidly high expectations and disapproving attitudes had done to their children. Slowly, they made the changes that finally revolutionized their family, and eventually Dan collected the courage to return home. What he found were open arms and tears of remorse for the pain those parents had so unwittingly inflicted. It took time but gradually Dan believed the changes, and his visits with me and the family eventually released the anger and pain he had known for so long.

In all too many cases, the break never occurs in the vicious cycle of pain, anger, retaliation, and separation that Dan and his family experienced. I feel immense hope, however, for any family who will face the facts regarding their broken relationships. With help they can gain the insights that will change the attitudes and impart the understanding that will heal those painful fractures, just as Dan and his family did.

–14–
HEALING THROUGH AWARENESS AND RESPONSIBILITY

No matter what the needed change may be, you must first become aware of that need if you are ever to make those changes. It took literally years for Dan's parents to recognize their family's problems. Until that time, the toxins of their disapproving, negative attitudes and behaviors continued to damage every relationship within that family. Once they understood, their basic, underlying love prompted the healing process that ensued.

The brief breaks in parent-child warmth, as in the child who did not want to clean his room, can be solved quickly and need never result in a lasting separation like Dan's.

Steps That Mend

No matter what the cause of a disturbed relationship, its cure must involve the following steps:

1. *A clear awareness of the existence of the problem* and what it is: failure of communication, unrealistic expectations, basic dislike of the other person (your child), excessive anger and disapproval in discipline, or your own individual interpretation.

2. *An unbending determination to solve the problem* and reestablish your loving relationship.

3. *Finding the courage to accept your own faults* as part of the problem and to change.

4. *Seeking help.* This too demands courage of a strong sort. It may be far easier to bumble along, trying to be strong enough to solve your own problems, but making repeated mistakes. There is strength in the ability to admit that you don't have all the answers and asking for guidance.

5. *Finding the tenacity to stick with the problem* until it is really resolved. I have seen so many parents work on an issue very well for a while, but they fail to stick with it through temporary failures until the desired change becomes permanent. One psychiatrist I know believes that *it takes at least one month of efforts to change for one year of time spent in old habits.*

Any worthwhile change takes time, energy, and involves risks. If you need to make some changes to prevent or mend serious rifts in your relationships, let me cheer you on! You and your child will be so glad you did it.

Rectifying Misunderstandings

In the Introduction, I shared with you my own painful experiencing of a broken relationship with my mother. I hope I made it quite clear that this failure was not due to her being a bad mother, or even my being a bad child (though I often thought she was and *very* often felt as if I were!). It was due entirely to my failure to understand why I had to lose my special, youngest-child position to a baby sister for whom I had never asked. Conversely, our failed relationship was complicated by my mother's inability to comprehend my position. She unconsciously expected me to feel delighted to have the baby sister she had wanted as a child. Many other misunderstandings fit into the rift that widened for years between the two of us.

And so it was that both of us missed so much intimacy and warmth—simply because of a mutual misunderstanding. If we had only known of a family counselor, we could have prevented those years of a damaged relationship.

After my mother's funeral service, our family followed her flower-laden casket out of the church. Oblivious to those who had kindly come to share our mourning, I mused as I walked down the aisle, "When I see Mother again, I know we will finally understand each other."

That thought may well have been planted in my mind by the heavenly Father as a prophetic message. Some ten years later, I began to learn how to resolve problems with a loved one, even when that person is no longer there to discuss them.

In a very private time, I sat quietly thinking (for the first time) of what I really had needed and wanted from my mother. Mentally I clarified those needs as pointedly as I could. I closed my eyes and imagined her sitting near me. I could easily envision her silver hair, shoulders bent with the arthritis that plagued her, and the loving expression so common to her. Why, I wondered, could I never find the words to say to her when she was still with me?

After finishing all of my wishes, needs, and feelings, I moved to the chair where, in my imagination, my mother was sitting. I tried to recapture the essence of her personality as I thought, *What would Mother say to me if she really were here, now?*

Something akin to a miracle suddenly took place in my emotions and raced instantly to my mind! As I tried in this semitangible manner to understand my mom, I suddenly saw the whole issue. As a child, I had felt that Mother no longer loved me. As a result, I began to behave in a hurt, sullen fashion, and I began to see myself as an ugly, unlovable child. Suddenly I realized that I was wrong on both counts.

My mother simply had not realized how lonely and rejected I felt. She wanted only to be a good mom, and to see all of her children loving one another would have verified her excellence. As a mother, I could identify with that wish.

But even more clearly there came to my awareness the certainty of my mother's love for me. She wanted me to grow up to be unselfish, responsible, and loving. How could a truly caring mother want less for any child?

In seeing that Mom had truly done the best she could, I finally understood her—and believed in her love. Then I could forgive her—and finally, also forgive myself. A strange sense of peace overcame my old grief, and a stream of tears washed from my heart the pain and resentments of all those years.

Interestingly, I had not even been aware of feeling that Mom hadn't loved me. Yet the relief of the revelation of how much she did care revealed to me that I had, in fact, felt rejected by her. It is exciting now to contemplate the reunion I know Mother and I will experience in our "life after life." We will, indeed, understand one another, and in understanding our love will flow again.

Be assured, parents, that it is never too late to mend a broken relationship!

Clarifying Misinterpretations

When I experienced a troubled relationship with my daughter, misinterpretations were rampant on both sides. Kathy felt that I was being too easy on her in those turbulent adolescent years. When she commented, "Mother, I don't think you yell at me enough," I know she felt that my failure to do so meant I was too busy to notice her tendency to rebel.

What I actually intended was to protect her from the sort of scoldings that had made my life as a child so miserable. It was essential, however, *that I understood how I seemed to her*, before I could interpret my real intentions.

It took some comprehensive listening and honest thinking before I could interpret my daughter's angry words, "You're so smart! You should know you can't treat me like a four-year-old when I'm fourteen!" Had I simply reacted in anger to her words, our relationship could have been seriously broken—perhaps permanently.

Thanks to my own childhood experiences, I had determined to have a positive, loving, and honest relationship with my children. And due to that commitment, I refused to settle for anger, so I endured the pain of facing my failures. I was able, then, to accurately interpret Kathy's words and face the truth in them. It was the pain beneath the anger that I had to understand.

The steps it takes to correct misinterpretations of another's words, attitudes, or actions are these:

1. *You must remember the facts.* Contrary to popular opinion, people do *not* say, in anger, what they feel most deeply. The anger always covers underlying pain.

2. *You must endure the painful revelation of your own mistakes.* To think that I had hurt my child's heart or damaged her life

was excruciatingly painful to me, but I could not make the necessary changes until I faced that.

3. *You must be honest and open enough to admit to your child that you were at fault.*

4. *You will also need to be patient enough to wait for your child to see and admit where he or she was also wrong.* (Children usually come to this point much more quickly than adults do!)

5. *You will need to learn to think more broadly and deeply so you can interpret your child's heart as clearly as his ideas and behaviors.*

6. *It will help immensely if you will learn to develop a curious mind more than a judgmental attitude, and to keep any expectations you have as positive as possible.*

7. *As in all good decisions, stick with the new, positive, honest plan.* Hanging in—with love—you will win!

Correcting Mistaken Identities

Billy. For three consecutive years, Billy had antagonized his classmates, challenged his teachers, and limited his successes in school. As I confronted his angry face again, I literally ached for this little boy who seemed so frustrated. In past years, I had analyzed the triangulated family in which he lived. His mother was heroically struggling to provide, alone, for him and his older sister. Janie was an excellent student, a great help to their mother, and a model sibling. Billy didn't much care for her angelic ways because they showed up his "badness" all the more. Somehow, I knew I had to find some means of helping not only Billy, but his mom as well.

Once more, I reviewed with this troubled mother the evolution of Billy's difficulties. His father's leaving was painful, but Billy seemed to have worked out his grief and anger over that. He had always resented his sister's successes, but Mother was trying to point out his achievements (few as they were!) to help him feel better.

There was, in this interview, such a clear-cut and negative difference in Mother's attitude toward Billy as contrasted with Janie, that I suddenly glimpsed a new facet to this old problem. I asked

Mom to review for me some of her childhood experiences. How had her father disciplined her? And what was her relationship like with her own mother?

She recalled a warm, supportive mother, and her eyes glowed with the love of that relationship. But as she described her father, her soft blue eyes turned to steel and her voice became harsh. She looked quite like she did when we talked about Billy. Next I asked, "And of whom does Billy remind you in that early family of yours?" Mother hesitated not one second as she announced, "Why he's the spitting image of my dad!"

With hardly a word from me, Mother quickly understood that she had been displacing on Billy her old hurts and anger toward his grandfather. Without previously recognizing it, she had, by her attitude, encouraged Billy to become increasingly like the person with whom she had vainly struggled so long ago.

It required only a little more counseling for this perceptive, loving mother to separate her old, negative feelings for her gruff father from the son who did resemble him. The more clearly she identified Billy as his own unique self, the less tension and irritation she felt toward him. She became free to understand, accept, and love him as never before. Billy not only welcomed the new relationship with his mom, but also he learned to feel good about who he was. His schoolwork and social adjustment became so excellent, I have not needed to see him again for some years.

Tearing Down Your Defenses

In order to form any healthy relationship, you must recognize not only your weaknesses, but also your strengths. The more you become acquainted with yourself as a whole person, the more I trust you will recognize that you are a basically decent person. And since you are a lovable and capable (though not perfect) person, you really do not need those problem-causing defenses:

Denial. Instead of trying to convince yourself that you did not make any mistakes (thereby eliminating any chance to correct them), go ahead and admit them. Everyone makes mistakes—little ones, big ones, downright stupid ones. But by realizing your basically healthy motives, you can simply own up to the fact of your goofs, discern why you erred, and learn to avoid such mistakes in the future. You are certain, of course, to make other mistakes, but you can even more quickly rectify them as you learn how to do that. Apologizing quickly and learning to stop repeating hurtful acts will inevitably mend and strengthen your relationships. Remember, you must replace those old mistakes with new and better habits that have been described in Parts I and II.

Rationalizing. Remember that people use this defense when they feel (or even fear) the disapproval of others. It is always right to sense misunderstandings and to interpret more accurately your actions or words. However, going beyond this sort of direct correction of poor communication puts you at risk for rationalizing. By believing in your own good intentions and deep-down honesty, you need not fear others' opinions and you will not need to use this defense.

Furthermore, rationalizing is a means of giving one's self certain permissions that are, in fact, not right. You may, for example, have had a very hard day at work and wish you did not have to play with your children or attend an evening activity with them. You can make yourself believe that, in fact, your evening to rest is far more essential than their needs or interests. Now, rarely, that may be true, but usually their fair share of your interest and energy is absolutely essential to your relationship with them.

The answer obviously is to take a few minutes to rest and then discipline yourself to enter into their plans with genuine enthusiasm. You can do this by using the power of choice to do one of three things: 1) Stick with your old habit of dishonestly rationalizing a selfish choice to "do your own thing"; 2) martyrishly pay attention to your children but resent every minute of it; 3) remember that your time with your children is relatively short, and you can choose to make it happy and loving by willingly giving yourself and your time to them.

Displacement. Taking out your frustration with one person on another, safer one is another form of dishonesty. While it may not be safe to vent your hostile or hurt feelings directly with a co-worker or friend, you can at least express these emotions clearly to yourself and usually to your family. It can be most comforting to relate some of your problems to your spouse and even (in general terms) to your children. By doing this, you will be letting them know you are not upset with them. You can also enable them to show their love and concern for you by asking specifically for some quiet time, a short back rub, or a listening ear. Think carefully of what you need for your special problem and ask for that. If you don't take unfair advantage and ask too much or too often, it will strengthen your relationship. I predict it will also enable you to face those issues with greater strength.

Reaction Formation. Going from one extreme to the other is something of the opposite of displacement. Instead of taking out your feelings on the wrong person, you repress them and work hard to find the protection of opposite emotions. You may feel very angry with your child who is rude and selfish—so angry, in fact, that you are afraid you might hurt him or her. By acting extremely patient, kind, and "loving," you can avoid the anger and the danger of abusing your child. But you will also miss the healthy discipline that child needs in order to stop the rudeness and selfishness.

Furthermore, your child will sense your lack of genuineness and will vaguely realize he needs your correction. To change this destructive pattern demands that you find the ideal point of intervention in your child's bad behavior early on, and that you learn to teach him in love (and yet with firmness) so you need not risk the excessive anger.

Such direct, clear, wise tactics will create a climate of trust between you and your child. Your relationship will be all the stronger because you know your anger means that correction is needed and your love will make that change in a manner that will help your child to be a better person.

Straightening Your Crooked Thinking

When my friend realized she was parenting her children as if she were their sister instead of their mother, she had some changing to do. Of course, her realization was the most important element in that change, but here are some additional steps she took:

She had to change her inner sense of identity. Believe me, that was truly difficult! From earliest childhood, she had been Daddy's special little girl. Unwittingly, Daddy had encouraged her to stay childlike by responding affectionately when she was "cute," by overprotecting her, and by his failure to *expect* her to become a mature person.

In addition to those childhood patterns, my friend married a man who also adored her little-girl charm. He, like her dad, unconsciously kept the payoff coming and encouraged her immaturity. As time went by, her husband found her childish temper more and more unpleasant, but he could tolerate that as long as her charm returned.

It was with their children that the supply of the so-called charm finally ran out. The demands for sacrifice, energy, giving, and consistency soon drained the bit of maturity this really likable person had acquired. She treated her children as if she were one of them—yelling, retaliating, or retreating in long periods of pouting.

Seeing her children develop potentially devastating personality problems, finally motivated my friend to change. What a struggle it was to give up the fixation on her "cute" self-image. Relinquishing the "Daddy" type of relationships she had enjoyed with her father and her husband meant that she had to become self-reliant, self-disciplined, and in charge of both her actions and reactions—no small task! But her family life was slowly transformed as she laboriously (if late!) grew up.

The next step: to make any lasting change in life also demands the simple but boring chore of breaking old habits. For a person who has traditionally depended on Daddy, this is especially difficult because she doesn't believe, at first, that she can (or even should be expected to) do such a difficult task.

During the woman's habit-breaking phase she often needed to have help. She would ask a friend, or even her family members, to remind her of times when she fell back into old ways. When she became especially discouraged she sought professional counseling. But she meant business and let nothing deter her from her goal.

Finally, even as she was giving up her old patterns of immaturity, she was searching for her new identity and way of life. To do so, she began to observe other women with new vision. What was it that made them stronger, more self-reliant, wiser? From some women she learned how to be more giving and unselfish. In others, she found a role model for controlling her wishes and practicing logic in making all kinds of decisions. She learned to ask for help of a different sort than ever before—help for "being" rather than in "doing."

Within herself, of course, this intelligent woman had to eventually find the determination and courage to face the loss of her excessive childishness and submit to the delayed grief over giving up its advantages. She finally became the wise, generous, and self-disciplined mother who could form a truly joy-filled, healthy parent-child relationship.

Whatever your particular area of distorted thinking and perception may be, you, too, can change. And change you must, if you want to mend your broken parent-child relationship. True enough, your child will need to change too, but one of you must begin. It's truly gratifying to realize that you, the parent, have become wise and insightful enough to initiate the change and make the corrections that will restore the bonds between you and your child, their original *love*-liness!

Breaking the Family Triangle

Earlier I described a family in which the father and daughter had developed a coalition that left out the mother and set her in competition with her daughter. No one was happy in such a situation, but at first, no one was clearly aware of its presence.

As is nearly always the case, it took pain to clarify the problem's very existence. This mother found herself feeling the hurt of loneliness at being left out of the growing intimacy of father and daughter. She sensed her husband's increasing permissiveness that was spoiling their child and creating resentments in her own heart.

In this situation, the problem really was focused on the father, but it was the mother's awareness that initiated the needed changes. In today's mental health climate, we talk and write a great deal about clarifying whose is the problem and avoiding trying to solve those dilemmas that belong to someone else.

When there is a family triangle, however, this philosophy may be misleading. As a matter of fact, this situation becomes everyone's problem. The one who first admits and faces up to the issue may be the key to solving it for everyone.

It is so essential that this be done with care, love, and wisdom. Reacting in anger can be felt by the others as jealousy and may drive them even closer to each other and away from you. It can lessen the opportunity to correct the imbalances and stop the unhealthy interactions.

Stopping the Competition. Here are the suggestions I offer if you believe there is a triangle in your family:

1. *Gain control over your anger, hurt, and fear so you can think clearly.* One way to achieve your control is to verbalize your feelings, recognize the specific events that prompt them, and begin to face the fact that you can make some good changes take place.

2. *Write down some of your emotions and the events that precipitate them.* Make sure that what you *think* is happening is, in fact, *accurate.* An insecure person may misinterpret interactions or overreact to them, so you need to step back and be objective.

3. *Seek a truly trustworthy person to serve as a sounding board.* In case you have misperceived the situation, such outside help can be immensely clarifying and healing and could prevent unnecessary family unheaval.

4. *Do not hesitate to seek competent professional counsel at this point.* You would not hesitate to see a physician for a severe physical pain. It is equally helpful to see a counselor to help you evaluate emotional pain.

5. *If you, your friend, and/or your counselor decide there is not a serious problem, set about strengthening your relationships with your family.* Learn to love yourself more confidently and hence become secure.

6. *If, however, you all agree there is a real problem, set about confronting it.* You will handle this best by being honest but as self-controlled as possible.

Confronting a Real Problem. Privately discuss with each of those involved your evaluation of the problem. It is best to use examples that are clear but not so painful that you dissolve in tears or erupt in anger. Stay definite and logical but kind.

You are certain to experience concern for your child and spouse as well as pain at being excluded and even put down by them. Be sure to express these feelings and any others you may experience; but in this case, you are likely to find that talking honestly *about* these emotions is wiser than displaying them openly.

Own up to your mistakes in this situation. It will take some uncomfortable introspection to discover your faults, but doing so will greatly hasten the solution.

Once you recognize that you have been too restrictive (allowing your spouse's permissiveness to get out of balance), or that you have withdrawn too much in order to protect yourself, or whatever other faults you will discover, discuss these openly. You will, of course, want to have a plan for breaking such habits. Make this commitment clearly.

Count on the original, basic love you each have for the other and believe that they want to change as much as you do. Ask each one what they will do to help so that change comes about. Work out, in other words, a joint contract or plan to break the hurtful patterns that have been formed and create better ones.

Be patient. Such triangles do not form overnight and they certainly will not change quickly. Each of you will fall into old habits from time to time. When that happens, encourage each other rather than condemning or criticizing.

Be sure to verbalize your appreciation for even the smallest efforts to correct this problem. And keep a positive attitude toward yourself—carefully avoiding self-pity or blame. You and the triangle can change!

This example has been that of a father and daughter pitted against the mother. It is equally possible for a mother and son to triangulate against a dad, a father and son to gang up on a mother, or a mother and daughter against dad. A psychologist friend of mine insists he has even seen one spouse and a pet take sides against the other spouse. If you grew up in a family that practiced such methods of relating, you are a likely candidate to fall into such a habit yourself. Let me remind you, no matter how difficult it is, *you can change!*

Another aspect of triangulation is that in which one parent and a child compete not for the affection but for the time and attention of the other parent. Such competition will certainly prevent or break a healthy parent-child relationship.

Time of Bonding. In most families, I believe, there is a period of time after the birth of a baby when the maternal instincts cause mothers to focus exclusively on the child. Such attention creates strong, positive bonding between mother and child. But it all unwittingly excludes Dad.

It is almost inevitable during these times that dads feel lonely and rejected at first but angry and even vengeful later on. A father who will find it difficult to admit such tender, lonely feelings is almost certain to resort to other activities to fill the void and to prove the self-worth he actually doubts. He may extend work hours or bring work home; he may spend time on sports or hobbies; or he may develop other relationships. Whatever his potluck solution, the basis for the problem is competition with his own children for his wife's attention.

In order to correct this problem and mend the missing or damaged parent-child relationship, there must be mutual understanding by both spouses. Fathers must recognize the instinctive nature of a mother-child relationship and know that it does not intend to exclude him, nor does it mean his wife no longer loves him.

Mother, in turn, must recognize the need to set some limits on her child care and must include her husband in parenting. Many fathers drop out of parenting because they feel inept and unsure of how to father! Mothers really need to understand that while men need some guidance in looking after a child, they rarely tolerate criticism and almost never bear ridicule. They are highly likely to avoid helping if these should happen.

Mothers must budget some time to enjoy their husbands and to work toward the strengthening of the marriage bonds. Then both husband and wife will be secure enough to give to their child the ingredients required for strong parent-child relationships.

The other type of competition is that restricted to a parent and a child. It may be of the same sex or the opposite, but the rivalry is intense, almost always it is unconscious, and it can seriously mar the parent-child relationship.

I have described the coach who could not allow his son to quite "make it" in his sport. Their relationship has never, to my knowledge, been mended because of the intense pain in the son. His father's disapproval, in his mind, turned to total rejection, and he decided to avoid his dad as much as possible. How sad that the man never did recognize his role in the estrangement. From his perspective, the son was too embarrassed at his failure to face him.

Another example of parent-child competition is one I have seen repeatedly. This type can be practiced by either parent, but I have seen it more commonly in mothers and daughters. It is typified by this example:

Cheryl. At fifteen she was a daughter any parent would have wished for. Her complexion was flawless, her blond hair shone with vitality and good care, her developing figure was the envy of her friends. Her naturally effervescent personality, however, was slowly changing. She was moody and often spoke rudely to her mother. Furthermore, her grades were slipping, and the school counselor was concerned about her impudent attitude toward her teachers.

As Cheryl and I talked, it soon became evident that her problem was quite clear to her, but its solution was not so simple. She described her irritation and embarrassment with flashing blue eyes and flushed cheeks. Every time she had friends in her home, and especially when there were boys in the group, her mother seemed to take over the conversation, leaving Cheryl feeling like an outsider.

"Why, Mom even tries to dress and talk like us teenagers!" Cheryl cried. "I don't want her to be like we are and I sure don't like the way she treats my boyfriends. In fact, I guess I don't like any adults right now!" And Cheryl was right; she had come to see adults as invading her turbulent teen world. Since they were becoming part of that world she had no anchoring spot to which she could turn when the waters were very rough. How confusing!

It's a great advantage to be a family counselor because one can gradually put together the entire, complex puzzle. So when I saw Cheryl's mother, I could understand so much more. She, too, was an attractive woman who, indeed, was desperately trying to be as young and glowing as her daughter. But the twenty years difference in age had etched their lines in her face, dulled her hair, and robbed her of the vitality reserved for the young.

Tragically, she had failed to recognize and develop the inner beauty that is found in wisdom and is achieved by facing the realities of life with courage and positive attitudes. So this mother was unknowingly trying to relive her youth through identifying with her daughter's friends. Her competition was destroying their relationship.

Vicki. She lay down her paintbrush and surveyed the canvas with a critical eye. The clouds hovering over the prairie scene she was creating were just a bit too light. As she turned away for a moment, we chatted about her developing skills as an artist.

Thoughtfully she asked, "Doctor Grace, do you think my mother resents my work? She's such a good artist, but I have a feeling she is afraid I'll be better than she is."

All too often such a possibility becomes reality. Parents raise children who very often rather worship them. When their relationship is warm and respectful, the parent becomes accustomed to the child's admiration and depends on it too much as a source of intimacy. They never quite make that transition from parent-child to friend-friend.

For Vicki to mend the weakened relationship with her mother was not really difficult. First, she reviewed with me the reasons for the fear of her mother's jealousy. They seemed logical and accurate. Knowing her mother, I next suggested she frankly discuss with her the attitudes that had aroused Vicki's fears. Fortunately her mother could face the unconscious feelings that had, in fact, come from her fear of changing roles with her adult child. She was, honestly, delighted by her daughter's talent and wanted her to know the highest success that was possible.

Rather than staying in competition, these two women became allies. Each could be the other's most loving and honest critic. They developed a collaboration that enhanced the excellence of both—and brought them to a new depth in their personal relationship.

The root of most such parent-child competition lies in the insecurity of the parent. For reasons related to their own childhood bonds with their parents, these moms or dads are afraid. And their fear is not actually that of being outdistanced by the child's achievements, but it is the fear of being emotionally abandoned by that child—no longer loved, respected, and needed.

−15−
UTILIZING THE TRAITS OF HEALTHY RELATIONSHIPS

Now let us return to those original characteristics of healthy parent-child relationships discussed in Part I. In exploring them from another perspective, I hope you will discover some ideas that will make it possible to mend any broken relationships you may have.

Creativity

Sometimes it is extremely helpful to return to the very beginnings of a relationship to rediscover its strengths.

Try to remember the weeks and months during which you and your spouse anticipated the birth of your child—the time when you created that tiny, new life. Can you recapture your excitement? Remember the dreams and hopes you shared for him or her. Recreate those early scenes in the hospital nursery and especially the times you watched that miniature body move and stretch—the tiny fingers that clung so trustingly to yours and the pink toes that wiggled when you kissed them.

Allow your memories to move along through the baby's life as if you were watching home movies of his development. Be especially alert to the point in his life when you first felt some anxiety or anger. Try to recapture the events that caused your concern. Could it have been when he began to resemble that harsh, stubborn sibling or parent who made your life so unhappy at times? Perhaps you, as do so many parents, saw in her some of your own traits—ones that have caused problems for you. Or maybe he resembles his father, who has not always been the easiest person with whom to live!

Whatever the reason, in realizing it, work hard to understand that that little child did not deliberately learn or practice those traits that have troubled you, so forgive him or her and completely let go of those old feelings.

As you are free from old, nearly forgotten resentments or worries, begin to observe your child with new eyes. From this different perspective, explore this child's abilities and commend her for those. Stop being critical of her weaknesses, but in creative ways try to help her strengthen those weak spots.

In your efforts to establish a new relationship, be creative. Instead of lecturing, try listening. Learn to ask questions for which you do not already have answers. And hear the replies without defensiveness—with your heart.

As you face your mistakes that have all too often created pain rather than trust, admit those errors. Only then can you offer the healing of a genuine apology. Let me remind you that only when you recognize your failures can you change your ways to better ones.

If you're not very comfortable with your communications skills, try writing notes. This creative means of communicating has some distinct advantages. It allows you to express emotions without embarrassment. It permits you to make explanations without defensiveness. It enables you to begin to overcome your shyness or reserve in a controllable manner.

Doing an extra service for your child is another example of creativity. Most parents find it difficult to get their children to clean their rooms and even suffer broken relationships over such a small task. Imagine once in a while that you choose a time when your child is extra hassled and the room a real mess! What might happen if you lovingly cleaned that room and left a note saying: I KNOW YOU'RE REALLY BUSY THIS WEEK AND I WANT YOU TO KNOW I UNDERSTAND HOW STRESSED YOU ARE. I THOUGHT A CLEAN ROOM, FULL OF MY LOVE, MIGHT HELP YOU THROUGH THE WEEK!

Fixing a special meal, doing a few extra lovetasks, showing your caring—these are ideas that can recreate your originally loving relationship.

Nurturing

Just as feeding your tiny baby got him off to a good start in life, so proper nurturing can restore a marred relationship.

The ingredients of good nourishment for a starving relationship are not really too difficult to understand. They are not, however, so easy to put together.

Facing Up. First, you will need to get order in your disorganized, mixed-up emotions. Face your hurts, resentments, and the guilt you are likely to have rationalized away. Only when you admit these uncomfortable feelings can you even begin to change them. Take each experience of pain and anger, thoughtfully collecting facts that will give you complete information about that child. Open your mind and heart to fully understand his or her side of that episode as well as your mistakes. Then forgive yourself *and* your child.

You may only need to do this exercise within yourself to become free of those negative feelings, but you may want to discuss some of your discoveries with your child. It can be immensely healing to your relationship for your child to hear you admit your failures. Your love must be clean—free from ambivalence in order to be convincing.

Priorities Check. Next, you will need to rearrange your priorities. Many fractured relationships are due to neglect. And such neglect is directly related to the order of your values. Putting personal achievements ahead of your child's basic needs is bound to cause trouble. Business success can crowd out time for your child's needs. And the search for pleasure is certain to detract from the focus on your child that he or she deserves. When you use your child's successes as evidence of your greatness as a parent, you may be sure your priorities are in disorder!

When you have established some honest and sensible order to your values and their priorities as well as in your emotions, you will be ready to take action. And be careful to avoid impulsive repairs to the "nutritional" mistakes, until your attitudes and feelings are healthy!

Make a Time Commitment. When you are ready, make a specific time commitment for your child and keep it. Even if that time is not appreciated at first, and you may feel it's not working, stick with it. Waiting an hour a day for a week or more, with your child avoiding you, is well worth it when at last he or she does admit the need of your help. Such waiting can be a reminder of the way your child felt when you were too busy for her!

"Merriment Doeth Good." Begin to add the ingredient of humor to your recipe. Taking events too seriously can make life a burden when it needs to be a joy. In most situations, a creative mind can find or inject just enough laughter to make a lesson easier to learn, or heal a hurt more rapidly.

Sharing. Sharing your experiences and your reaction to those events is a basic ingredient of a nurturing relationship. As you reveal the challenges of your life and how you have met them, your child will be growing in his insights and coping skills. Even when you have made mistakes, facing and overcoming those can help your child acquire the skills to cope with his or her mistakes. Best of all, you will be revealing the real person you are and will cement your child's respect and affection.

Spiritual Life. Nurturing your child's spiritual life is essential to his overall wholeness. To do this demands sharing your own religious beliefs and spiritual values. Feeding your child's spirit can gently motivate you to grow in your own life, and as you and your child grow, your own soul will expand.

Don't Forget the Mind. Intellectually, as well, you will benefit by reading, thinking, and discussing significant topics with your children. The advantages will be enhanced by inviting their ideas and responses to your own. The perceptions of children have a simple wisdom that is truly profound. Test it out, and let your child know how much you respect his ideas—even when you may not agree with them.

Once you get the right recipe, nurturing your child can be fun—enriching to your own life, and strengthening to your relationship.

Protecting

To repair a weak or broken relationship is a sensitive and delicate job. As healing begins to take place, you will find it easy for even a slight backsliding into old habits to do further damage. So it is even more important to be protective in repairing than in building a relationship initially.

From Your Mistakes. You will need to protect your child from your own mistakes. While it is important to maintain a clear sense of what is right and wrong, you must avoid harshness or put-downs. Teach your child (and learn, yourself, if you need to) that he is a special, loved person—even when he misbehaves. Keep your unconditional love so evident that even when he acts the worst, your child *knows* you accept him as a person.

On the other hand, make the disapproval of any behavior that is unworthy of him quite clear. Tell him what is unacceptable about his actions and what you expect. Or better still, help him decide what to do instead. Be sure to notice any efforts to improve and give unqualified praise for trying.

From False Information. Your child also needs protection from false or misleading information. Many young people break off relations with the best of parents because their friends' parents are too permissive. A young person's biggest job is that of establishing his independence and finalizing his personal identity. It is tempting for young people to believe that families who allow a great amount of freedom are ideal. If you set even normal limits, then your teenagers are likely to believe you are too strict and they will rebel.

If this has happened in your family, I suggest that you try to help your child see the need for a balance in freedom and responsibility. Often, one of those "liberated" friends gets into trouble due to the lack of parental protection. Such an object lesson finally makes thoughtful young people grateful for their parents' guidance. Clear teaching, kindly attitudes, but firmness in the limits that must be set will win such struggles and strengthen your relationship in the final analysis.

From Child's Impulses. Often a child, or adolescent, will desperately need protection from their own impulses. Parents who let their children get by with too much impudence or impulsiveness will eventually lose the respect of those offspring.

To correct this mistake requires your absolute certainty of the need for a change. When this is clear, sit down with your child and kindly discuss the danger in such habits. These dangers include the loss of friends, personal embarrassment after the episode is past, and the likelihood of growing up to be an obnoxious spouse or parent. Seek to help your child become aware of the problems he/she is creating and suggest that you work out a plan together to break those old habits. Help him learn to verbalize his feelings—before they explode—in a positive, constructive manner.

Such a plan, by the way, must include enhancing each child's awareness of feelings early on. He/she will need to learn a vocabulary that clearly and adequately expresses them. It must also involve an understanding of the events that prompt such intense reactions, and a decision regarding some action that will resolve the incident and prevent its happening again.

From Pampering. Finally, protect your child from your tendency to pamper him. If you have practiced such a habit, it will certainly impair your relationship with your son or daughter. Despite his taking advantage of your weaknesses and tendency to give in to his whims, and even despite his demanding such spoiling, he will not respect that. Deep within him, he will know such treatment weakens him and he will resent it.

You must break such habits if you are to gain the respect that is essential in a healthy relationship. To change this old habit, face, honestly, the likelihood that you have given in to this child for selfish reasons: it is easier to give in; it may be an unconscious attempt to relive your own youth; or it may be an effort to vicariously enjoy what you wanted and couldn't have; sometimes this pampering is a means of showing the world how generous you are—what a wonderfully kind parent!

Whatever your reason, give it up! Think clearly about the need for your child to experience the security of proper limits. Recognize the power of helping him accomplish tasks and complete projects if he is to achieve a healthy sense of self-worth. Teach him healthy pride in earning a privilege or acquiring an item he wants very much.

In paradoxical language, protect your child from your overprotectiveness, and you will have mended one more weak spot in your relationship.

Educating

Disciplining. Failure to teach your *young* child how to behave and to learn healthy attitudes may not seem to threaten your relationship. Later on, however, the weak spots in the very foundation of that relationship will become apparent. When you have not taken time to see to it that your little toddler learns obedience and respect, he is not likely to develop that suddenly in his teens. And you will not feel good about his disrespect then.

It is tempting to be permissive with children because they seem *happier* when they get their way, and so many parents only want to make their children happy. Such superficial happiness, however, is deceptive.

When the child has to face the real world of school, social demands, or (much later) a job, he will not possess the self-control that can enable him to do so successfully. Along the way, many children tell me they doubt their parents' honest caring when they allow them to get by with such misbehaviors or laziness.

Parents, even when your children act rebellious at your teaching and limit setting, be assured they need and even want it.

In repairing the weakness of permissiveness, let me remind you that teaching, while it *is* good discipline, is also much more. It is modeling an entire way of life that you believe in.

Be an Example. It is easy to drift into a life-style that is nonproductive, critical, or on the other hand, deceptively permissive. When you sit and watch TV every evening you are setting an example for your children that is risky. You are showing them how to be passive, uncreative, and empty of solid learning and thinking. Occasional TV programs, especially when you discuss the concepts that are portrayed, can be stimulating. But the constant practice of such an occupation allows you and your family to be robbed of priceless opportunities to teach them a healthy, positive life-style. By your example, be certain that you teach your children solid values, proper priorities, and logical thinking.

Decision Making. Share with your children the way you arrive at decisions. Much of successful living and relating comes from the ability to make wise choices and decisions—based on sound thinking rather than impulsiveness or taking the easy way out of a dilemma. When you must buy a new item for your home, for example, or replace a worn-out automobile, include your children in the discussion regarding that purchase. When the car needs washing or the house needs painting, simply and clearly describe to your child how you know it needs to be done—and that you are neither arbitrary nor bossy in asking that these jobs be done. Such decisions are necessary in one way or another almost every day. Faulty choices and even poor processing of information often cause trouble in relationships—but equally important is the ability to correct such mistakes or weak spots.

Being a good teacher regarding daily living is a beautiful opportunity for all parents. Here are some logical steps that will help you in educating your child:

1. *What are the basic facts about this forthcoming decision?* From bedtimes to big choices, like buying a new car, there are vital pieces of information you need.

2. *Separate these facts from your feelings about the situation.* You may feel too weary or discouraged to enforce study time for your child. The fact is, she needs to observe such a habit if she is to master her schoolwork.

3. *Make the proper decision that relates to those facts.* Be aware that at times you will think, or even say, "I know I ought to go and mow that tall grass. It will be too tall by next weekend." Or even, "I simply have to get this house cleaned!"

Unless, however, you actually command your muscles to move your body to take action, those jobs will not get done. You will discover that this thinking will work better: "At 2:30 this afternoon, I'm going to get this job done."

4. *Follow through.* No matter how superbly you collect facts, or how expertly you recognize those stubborn feelings, or even how efficiently you make your plans and schedules, nothing will happen until you actually take action.

These steps are extremely important in the most important of all decisions in broken relationships—that of facing up to the facts of the problem's very existence. It is you, the parent, who must initiate the action that will repair such painful fractures. As you follow through with the job of repairing, you will be teaching your child a priceless skill for living in love!

Categories of Teaching. Whether you know it or not, there are four categories you as parents will teach your children. By your attitudes and actions, even more than your words, you will be forming your child's beliefs in these basic areas of life:

1. *His self-concept.* Early in life, your child will learn to see and think of himself very much as you regard him. This fact brings clearly into focus the reason for being loving, affirming, and pleased with that child most of the time. It explains why your mode of training and teaching must be kind but firm and consistent.

2. *His concept of the world in which he lives.* While this view begins in the crib, it quickly enlarges to the family and then the community. What sort of world are you creating for your child? Is it chaotic and frightening? Is it confusing and frustrating? Or is it safe and consistent, resulting in security and successful living?

3. *His concept of others and how he relates with them.* The patterns you establish in relating with each other, Mom and Dad, are those you are certain to extend to your child. Be very careful to mend any inharmonious motifs in your family relationships. You can be both honest and kind in your communicating. It is possible to use self-control in establishing consistency so your child learns he can trust you to "be there" for his needs. You can make for yourselves and your child a safe, warm, inviting world. Much of such an environment will enter into your child's very personality. And he will carry its health and protection with him into the wide world outside your family!

4. *His concept of the heavenly Father.* Helping groups that clarify the universal need for each human being to depend on God have been highly successful. Alcoholics Anonymous, Narcotics Anonymous, and many others have developed a good degree of success in rehabilitating addicted people.

And much of that success depends on individuals' willingness to admit their need of that "Higher Power."

It will be so much easier for your child to avoid the heartache of chemical abuse and other failure patterns if he has grown up with kind, logical, and wise parents. His view of the heavenly Father is unconsciously weighted by his feelings about you. If, despite sound relationships, your child does rebel for a time, he is likely to return to you and to a positive life-style more rapidly because of your parenting skills.

If you have failed to be the sort of parent who makes it a joy for your child to trust God, don't despair! That's what this section of the book is about—mending broken relationships. If you will admit your shortcomings and, by God's guidance, get them corrected, you can still find that happy ending.

One of the greatest qualities you can teach your child is that of making needed changes. By your personal change and growth, you will be setting the unparalleled example your child needs.

As you learn to trust God and live as He would like to enable you to do, your child will also learn! What better gift could you give her?

I trust you will learn to feel very good about yourselves, parents. And then I hope you will correct past mistakes that have hurt your child and marred his self-concept. I hope you will learn to present to your child a picture of the world that keeps some optimism and hope alive in him. I want very much that the love and trust between you and your child will lay the foundation for healthy relationships with others. And most of all, may you, your child, and your personal world be encircled by the infinite love, power, and wisdom of God Himself!

Playing

We have already discussed how the tendency to keep life too serious can break a good relationship. Making even play itself a project that is too difficult destroys the very health it could create.

Humor. So sit back and take a good, long look at your family. How often do you laugh together? Is that laughter healthy and free? Or is it the cynical laughter that puts down another person or makes light of a really important value or concept? Do you confuse your child by smiling over some truly damaging—but *cute*—misbehavior?

If you have never developed the sense of humor that is truly healthy—even sanity-saving at times—I strongly urge you to set about finding how to do that. Learning this is not easy, but it is possible.

Your child is almost certain to have a supply of funny stories, and if you will allow yourself to relax, even the most serious of you will soon find the capacity to laugh. Let me warn you, it is easier at first to hold back your laughter. But I urge you to do the opposite—make yourself laugh even if the story doesn't seem funny. With such practice, you will discover or remember how to practice that merriment that "doeth good like a medicine" (Proverbs 17:22).

If you will open both your mind and heart, you will find that not only can you educate your child, but he will teach you the healing power of laughter and play. Imagine with me the difficulty in staying estranged from anyone with whom you can share laughter and play! It cannot be done.

Not only will the sharing of play and laughter strengthen a weak or ailing relationship, it will keep it healthy. And it will prevent many recurrent problems from becoming serious.

Perhaps your children are too old or too young to teach you how to laugh or play. As bad as too much TV is, there are always a few programs that are full of healthy fun. You will learn to recognize and respect the performers in such programs, and from them, too, you can learn to laugh.

Due to the cultural tendency toward cynicism, I would warn you that you must distinguish good, childlike fun from sarcastic humor. The latter always holds a barb that is intended to hurt someone. Avoid that!

Be Observant. Another source for learning to have fun is to observe other families. Find ways and time to observe a variety of families—in restaurants, parks, sports events, or church activities.

Wherever you find parents and children playing, talking, and laughing together, you will have an opportunity to learn.

I predict you will find some types of play that will feel right and natural to you while others won't fit you. Try out the ones that seem to be comfortable for you. Soon you'll be at ease with a truly healthy style of playing that will heal or prevent many hurts.

I strongly urge you dads and moms to schedule some time to play with each other. Keeping the fun of your marriage alive will set an example for your child's future. In the present, such happiness between you will provide great security for your child. So many children see the parents of their friends separating, and they worry whenever you have disagreements.

Conversely, when your child sees you displaying good humor and affection with each other, he or she will feel more confident and secure. So you see, everyone does benefit from that "merry heart"!

Releasing

Knowing when and how to begin to let go of a child is a difficult bit of information to acquire. There is an almost instinctive part of us parents that would like to hold our children close to us. We want to protect them; we fear we have failed as parents and try to hastily reconstruct better parenting skills; we believe that they have really learned nothing we've tried to teach and are certain to goof!

In our anxiety, we overreact, read too much into their looks and actions, and end up with severely damaged relationships, just when both the child and parent most need confidence.

Crucial Points. There are several stages of which you need to be aware. The first is at the point of a child's entering school—especially the *first grade.* Spending an entire day with an adult other than you, the parent, can be traumatic. That is especially true if you have not placed your child in day care or preschool.

If you can endure the pangs of doubt and sadness, and trust your child and his teacher, you will weather this separation successfully. If, however, you fear you have in some degree, at least, failed in your parenting, you may panic and unwittingly fall into overprotecting your child and taking sides with him against the teacher.

Such a possibility, sooner or later, will almost certainly result in resentment and estrangement from that child. Children feel weak and inadequate and often endure teasing by other children that results in pain, when a parent is overprotective.

Furthermore, taking sides with your child against a teacher spoils the necessary authority of the school. When a child recognizes no power beyond his own, he is certain to get into really serious power struggles or a character defect that can spoil his entire life.

The next vital stage in releasing your child is *at the entry into junior high school or middle school.* The latter is an increasingly popular movement in the USA and usually includes the fifth and/or sixth grades along with seventh and eighth.

In either event, your child knows that more independence and responsibility will be expected of him. He is likely to feel afraid of the newness and yet excited about the increased freedom he can explore. The finely tuned balance in letting go of your child so he can succeed in exploring and growing—and yet keeping some limits so he will not become wild—is difficult to find and maintain.

When such a balance has not been established, your relationship will suffer. Your child is likely to rebel in some degree, or on the other extreme, may be so dependent on you that he becomes a burden instead of a joy.

Learn From Your Child. The dramatic and profound change this era carries with it is exemplified by my own child. It was during her eighth-grade year that I was learning to be a more considerate and tactful mother. One evening I gently reminded her, "In a few minutes it will be time to turn off the TV and start your homework."

In retrospect, I can see that I made the unforgivable mistake of speaking as one would to a young child. Hence I could not blame her for exploding with, "Mother! You can't boss everything I do anymore! Even if you make me sit with my books, you should know you can't make me concentrate and learn. Besides, you know very well I keep my grades up, and I don't need you to tell me!"

Now almost all healthy children make such rude and hostile speeches at times. Rather than returning lecture for lecture or punishing them for disrespect, parents *need* to listen to them. In my adolescent's tirade, there was enough truth to keep my mind busy all evening digesting it! You will avoid damaging power struggles by truly hearing your children.

In case you haven't learned to listen, and your broken relationship reflects that, please try to change. What I did was face the facts and agree with my maturing child. In fact I could *not* force her to learn or even to study. Furthermore, I could see that I had helped her develop good study skills and I had demonstrated my pride in her excellence as a student.

What was infinitely more painful to me was facing the fact that she no longer needed my supervision. I really yearned to keep her close to me by encouraging her need of me! And that, you see, eventually would have crippled her development and ruined our relationship.

Interestingly, when I calmed down and logically discussed her comments, I could honestly agree with my child. Through that agreement, we came to a constructive contract: Kathy would take over the responsibility of her study habits, and I would enter into that area of her life only if the grades slipped significantly.

My confidence in her reliability and my own past parenting (even with its shortcomings) saved the day—and strengthened our relationship. If your bonds with your child are broken, try a bit of release, and see if you, too, will mend those fractures.

On Their Own. Perhaps the most difficult release of all times is that of sending your new adult son or daughter off to college or out of the nest to live on their own. In today's world, so ravaged by drugs, violence, and general lawlessness, that release is especially frightening!

In fact, the fear of release is due even more to the awareness of these external dangers than to the personal relationship problems. Even so, you must steel yourself and find the courage to cut the bonds and let go.

Sally. When Sally returned home after her first year of college, her mother (after much thought), sat her down for a talk. She reminded her daughter—and herself—that she had been several hundred miles away from home for nine months. Both of them had survived that and the young woman had studied hard and behaved well.

Now it was time, Mother stated, for her to show such an adult sense of responsibility at home. Together, they worked out the ground rules: Sally would help with the family laundry and the housecleaning when she could. She would tell her parents where she would be and about when she would be home at night.

In return, Mother would not quiz her and would avoid nagging or lecturing. She would trust Sally to treat the family with basic respect.

Later that summer, Sally and her mother were having lunch together. Abruptly Sally said, "I want to thank you, Mom, for trusting me this summer." A bit hesitantly she revealed, "Some of my friends like to drink beer. And sometimes they drink too much. I'm just glad I don't have to keep up with them—because I don't need to prove anything. Knowing you trust me has been so neat!"

You can imagine that mother's joy in her daughter's revelation. She had released her child—and in return, she gained a trusted adult friend!

Returning Point

Some of you are certain to feel that you have permanently muffed your interactions with your children. You are honest enough to face your mistakes and to recognize the problems. But you are pessimistic enough to believe there is no hope for repairing the breaks in your relationship. You feel that you have reached the point of "no return."

In travel, of course, there is such a point. When you are more than halfway to your destination, it would take longer and be more difficult to go back than to simply finish your journey.

But in mending broken relationships that rule does not apply. No matter how far you have traveled on life's journey, you may always stop off, reestablish contact, and repair the damage. It may demand swallowing some pride, or finding the time and energy to locate a lost child, or simply waiting and praying for his return. But honest love and reasonableness will win out.

Earlier I described how I had experienced healing in my troubled relationship with my mother. Even if you have lost a child through death, you can make your own peace with that child. I believe firmly in eternal life, so it makes great sense to work through those hurts, even if your child is not here to do so with you.

When you have released your child, some of you may heave a sigh of relief and believe that your responsibilities are over. Now I hope *your* relationships have not been a burden to you. But if they have, please try to rearrange things to allow room for change.

Role of Grandparents. Your adult children will always need you, and that can be fulfilling—but in increasingly intense ways, *you will be needing them.* Your grandchildren can bless you in an immeasurable degree if you will keep your home and heart open to them.

Yet many young parents find those doors locked. They are at a loss as to any means for opening them. If you are young parents or older grandparents, do not lightly ignore such estrangement.

Grandparents, you may be wary of the possibility of being used by your children for free child care or easy financial assistance in stressful times. Many grandparents have experienced such unfair demands by selfish, adult offspring.

Consider the fact that such selfishness may have arisen out of your being too permissive and spoiling them, or too busy and ignoring them. Now they may ignore you except when they desperately need you.

If you have contributed to such poor relationships, don't give up in guilt or despair! It's never too late to make amends. Just get clear in your mind where you were in error. Simply but sincerely offer an apology. And finally change your attitude and behavior so your adult children will be convinced that you are different.

Older Parents. Parents, you, too, can make a difference in mending broken bonds with your own parents. Be very careful to avoid taking advantage of them or using them. Keep a positive and loving attitude toward them, even when they may be disapproving or grumpy. Try to remember all the positive things about your childhood and remember to express appreciation for them at appropriate times. A little note on a thoughtful card can do wonders to change the feelings of those grandparents.

Whether they seem to welcome you or not, return to visit your parents regularly. If they do not seem to be excited to see you, don't stay long, and carefully avoid inconveniencing them. But do not give up the regular returning to those parents who raised you. In time, you may be surprised to find them mellowing.

I recall my psychologist friend whose mother somehow held out against responding to his affection for some twenty years. He gently, unrelentingly loved her—verbally by phone and physically during visits. Eventually she began to respond to his warmth and returned his affection. Love is too important to miss—whatever it takes of persistence and time, it's worth the investment.

Just be sure, parents, that you build of your home a place for returning. Keep the limits with which you can live very clear to your child and yourself. And keep the warmth, encouragement, and welcome for your children genuine.

Forgiving

All broken relationships demand forgiveness in order to be healed. Much had been written and spoken about this vital force in mending hurts. Rarely, if ever, however, have I found that such speakers or writers include one essential ingredient: it is simply *enough information to create profound understanding.*

By the very nature of estrangement, it is difficult to communicate. Therefore, the facts that could make such a difference often remain unknown. Do not let this happen to you! Take the risk of asking questions that will enable you to understand your child—or your parent. Let the person know that you are not just idly curious, but you are seeking to understand in order to restore that loving relationship. And then do allow that information to make a difference.

In psychiatry, therapists are commonly accused of putting the blame on the parents for all kinds of problems of their patients. Nothing could be further from the truth. In fact, many problems of my patients begin with hurts and misunderstandings that come from poor parent-child relationships. The therapist's task is to point out misconceptions the patient may have.

In my training days, I met regularly with a group of mothers. One of these women was experiencing double trouble—she was at odds with her daughter and had never gotten along with her mother.

I recognized that the trouble with her child had its roots in this mother's childhood. So we began to explore the traumatic events in her relationship with her mother. I asked her to tell me about her seemingly angry mother's early life. As she collected the facts about that period of time, this mother began to truly understand her mom.

The more profound that understanding became, the more complete was my patient's insight. One day in group, she broke into tears as she shared with us the fact that she finally could feel a deep compassion and warm love for her mother. Her words were engraved in my memory: "You know, Doctor Grace, when I finally understood my mother, I found it easy to forgive her. I believe I can even learn to love her!"

It was these words that awoke my lasting belief that forgiveness demands understanding. And understanding can come only from accurate information. Of course when that information lodges in an open mind and a sincerely caring heart, it creates forgiveness of the best kind!

Tenacity

It is truly difficult to mend broken relationships. It demands humility enough to face one's faults and guilt. It certainly requires a loving heart and an open mind.

But even more essential than these qualities is the *commitment to stick with the process.* The breaking of any parent-child relationship occurs over a long period of time as the result of a series of blunders—known or not. Let me assure you that repairing such breaks also takes time. Remember my friend's formula: It takes a month of counseling and serious effort to change the habits of a year of life.

If you have practiced being harsh and critical for twenty-five years, it will take just over two years to break that habit and form a new one. If this estimate is even close to an accurate fact, what it reveals is the necessity of sticking with the mending process. Only such tenacity will truly win.

Any relationship of real depth and honesty is almost certain to suffer damage from time to time. It is how you react to such harm that determines the eventual strength of the relationship.

You can give up and allow silent or even violent estrangement to permanently mar your love for each other; *or you can marshal your energy, intellect, and courage.* You can face the problems that threaten the joy between you and your child. When those problems have caused actual distance between you, don't wait. Carve out of each day time to review your communication and commitment. Assess the feelings you experience for each other.

Join me in my commitment. I try to never retire at night with any unresolved negative feelings for anyone. And if I sense that another person harbors hurts or anger with me, I make every effort within my power to create healing for that person.

May your relationships, too, be crowned with peace, joy, and love!

A PARENT'S PRAYER

Oh, Heavenly Father, make me a better parent.

Teach me to understand my children, to listen patiently to what they have to say and to answer all their questions kindly. Keep me from interrupting them, talking back to them and contradicting them. Make me as courteous to them as I would have them be to me. Give me the courage to confess my sins against my children and to ask of them forgiveness, when I know that I have done them wrong.

May I not vainly hurt the feelings of my children. Forbid that I should laugh at their mistakes or resort to shame and ridicule as punishment. Let me not tempt my child to lie and steal. So guide me hour by hour that I may demonstrate by all I say and do that honesty produces happiness.

Reduce, I pray, the meanness in me. May I cease to nag; and when I am out of sorts help me, oh, Lord, to hold my tongue.

Blind me to the little errors of my children and help me to see the good things that they do. Give me a ready word for honest praise.

Help me to grow up with my children, to treat them as those of their own age, but let me not exact of them the judgments and conventions of adults. Allow me not to rob them of the opportunity to wait upon themselves, to think, to choose, and to make decisions.

Forbid that I should ever punish them for my selfish satisfaction. May I grant them all their wishes that are reasonable and have the courage always to withhold a privilege which I know will do them harm.

Make me so fair and just, so considerate and companionable to my children, that they will have a genuine esteem for me. Fit me to be loved and imitated by my children.

With all thy gifts, oh, great Jehovah, give me calm and poise and self-control.

Garry Cleveland Myers, Ph.D.
Co-founder, HIGHLIGHTS FOR CHILDREN